Back-to-School

Grades 4–6

THE BEST OF The MAILBOX® Magazine

Great back-to-school ideas, activities, and reproducibles from the 1998–2002 issues of *The Mailbox*® magazine

- **Classroom Displays**
- **Organizational Tips**
- **Classroom Management**
- **Getting Acquainted**
- **Birthdays and Celebrations**
- **Parent Communication**
- **Open House**
- **Art Activities**

And much, much more!

Managing Editor: Debra Liverman

Editorial Team: Becky S. Andrews, Kimberley Bruck, Karen P. Shelton, Diane Badden, Thad H. McLaurin, Debra Liverman, Karen A. Brudnak, Sarah Hamblet, Hope Rodgers, Dorothy C. McKinney

Production Team: Lisa K. Pitts, Pam Crane, Rebecca Saunders, Jennifer Tipton Cappoen, Chris Curry, Sarah Foreman, Theresa Lewis Goode, Ivy L. Koonce, Clint Moore, Greg D. Rieves, Barry Slate, Donna K. Teal, Tazmen Carlisle, Amy Kirtley-Hill, Kristy Parton, Debbie Shoffner, Cathy Edwards Simrell, Lynette Dickerson, Mark Rainey

www.themailbox.com

Table of Contents

©2005 The Mailbox®
All rights reserved.
ISBN# 1-56234-640-7

Manufactured in the United States
10 9 8 7 6 5 4 3 2 1

Add a Little Fabric

For a quick decorating trick that will transform your classroom, head to your local fabric store. Buy fabric when it's on sale, and look for prints and solids that tie in with your teaching themes. Then use the fabric to back your bulletin boards. When a piece of fabric needs cleaning, just dip it into a sink of water and liquid soap, and then hang it on a hanger to drip-dry. For eye-catching bulletin board titles, place your letters front side down on the back of a piece of fabric; then laminate and cut out the letters. Not only does fabric brighten up a classroom, but it also never seems to fade, show staple holes, or tear.

Terry Schneider—Gr. 5
Clarkdale-Jerome School
Clarkdale, AZ

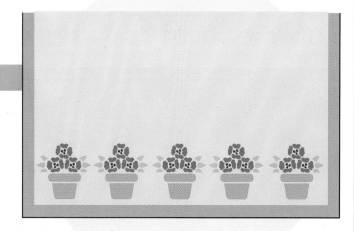

Reading Throne

Here's an inexpensive way to make students feel regal when they're reading! All you need is a white plastic lawn chair and two cans of gold spray paint. Spray-paint the chair outdoors and let it dry over-night. Hot-glue some jewels, rhinestones, or beads to the chair. If desired, add an inexpensive tie-on cushion. Now you have a special (and inexpensive!) chair for your reading center.

Michelle Curtis—Gr. 5
Preston Hollow Elementary
Plano, TX

Stencil It!

For an easy, inexpensive way to add color to your classroom, try stenciling! Stencil a simple border around a bulletin board, or have students make the border for you. Not only can you buy inexpensive stencils and craft paints at most discount stores, but you can also use the stencils over and over again.

Marti Bierdeman—Gr. 5
Bolin School
East Peoria, IL

Classy Classroom Curtains

Hide unsightly windows—and give students ownership of their classroom—with these easy-to-make curtains. Just follow these steps:

1. Cut large pieces of muslin to fit your windows.
2. Hem each piece two inches from the bottom. Also make a two-inch casing at the top. (If you don't sew, use iron-on bonding tape from a fabric store.)
3. Divide students into groups of three or four. Give each group a large sheet of butcher paper.
4. Assign each group a topic you're studying, such as the colonies, Egypt, or animals. Have each group draw a scene about its topic on the butcher paper. Encourage designs that have large items and are not too detailed.
5. When the designs are complete, give each group a curtain. Have the group use pencils to draw its scene on the curtain.
6. Have each group paint its scene with fabric paint.
7. When the paint is dry, outline the pictures in each scene with a wide-tip permanent marker.

If you can't hang the curtains permanently, use inexpensive tension rods. At the end of the year, draw a name from each group and reward that student with a curtain to take home!

Heather Eubank—Gr. 5
Willow Brook Elementary
Creve Coeur, MO

Swap Shop

One teacher's trash is another teacher's treasure, right? If you're wanting to replace some classroom decorations that you've been using for years, organize a schoolwide swap shop. Ask interested coworkers to gather items they'd like to trade. Then invite everyone to your classroom one day after school to swap decorations and ideas on how to use them. Everyone comes away with something new!

Julia Alarie—Gr. 6
Essex Middle School
Essex, VT

Shoebox Cubbies

Before the new school year begins, collect a class supply of shoeboxes. After school starts, have each student decorate the inside of a box with stickers and markers. Then use heavy tape to combine the boxes. Cover the outside of the boxes with wallpaper or Con-Tact paper. Use these shoebox cubbies for storage, as student mailboxes, or as display cases for items that kids bring to school to share.

Kimberly A. Minafo
Carmel, NY

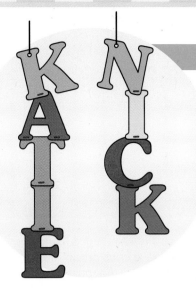

Name Mobiles

Colorful name mobiles make quite an impression when students enter your classroom at the beginning of the year. To make the mobiles, cut colorful construction paper letters for each student's name. Staple the letters of each name together vertically, punch a hole near the top of the first letter, add string, and hang the name from the classroom ceiling. Name mobiles make a striking display that students and parents alike just love!

Beverly Vest—Gr. 4
Slaughter Intermediate
McKinney, TX

Just a Few Bucks

Decorating on limited funds? No problem! Check out these nifty, thrifty ideas:

- Do you have an old countertop that needs a face-lift? Cover it with marble Con-Tact paper. Visitors to your classroom just might think you have a brand-new countertop!
- Buy some inexpensive sheets from a discount store and make curtains backed with Velcro strips. These curtains can be easily removed when blinds need cleaning.
- Are your posters and large bulletin board sets squeezed between cabinets? Eliminate this unsightly storage problem by storing the large items in an outdoor-size garbage can.
- Bring personal knickknacks from home. Baskets and air fresheners enhance the overall atmosphere of a classroom and give it a warm, welcoming feeling.

Terry Warner—Gr. 4
Brookview Elementary
Jacksonville, FL

Name Magnets

These eye-catching name magnets have tons of classroom uses! To make them, write each student's name on a small poster board rectangle and add a decorative sticker. Then cover the tag with clear Con-Tact paper and add a strip of magnetic tape to the back. Attach the magnets to your chalkboard and use them in the following ways:

- For daily lunch count, write the choices on the chalkboard. Then have each student place his nametag under his choice.
- To take attendance, have each student move his magnet to a specific area of the chalkboard when he arrives.
- When students need to choose from among several options, list the options on the board. Then have each student put her magnet under her choice.
- Use the magnets as chalkboard math manipulatives to create class graphs and teach fraction concepts.

Peggy O'Meara—Gr. 5
Cathedral of the Risen Christ School
Lincoln, NE

Matt Seitz	Matt Seitz	Matt Seitz
Matt Seitz	**Matt Seitz**	**Matt Seitz**
Matt Seitz	Matt Seitz	Matt Seitz
Matt Seitz	**Matt Seitz**	**Matt Seitz**

School Supply Labels

Get students organized before the new school year even begins! During summer, send home a letter to the parents of your new students. The letter should include a list of supplies the child will need for the upcoming school year. Also enclose several sheets of labels that have been personalized with the student's name in different sizes and fonts. Ask that the parent affix these labels to all of the student's school supplies before the child brings them to school. With this simple idea, students don't come to school with supplies they won't need or without necessary items. Plus you've eliminated the problem of lost pencils, assignment pads, and glue sticks!

Janice Barger—Gr. 5 Gifted
Moon Lake Elementary
New Port Richey, FL

Durable Hall Passes

Tired of remaking worn-out hall passes? These sturdy hall passes will stick around all year long. Ask a local paint store to donate several wooden stir sticks. Spray-paint the sticks and label each one with a different destination (library, office, bathroom, etc.). A small strip of magnetic tape attached to the back of each pass will keep it stuck to any metal surface until needed.

Paige Brannon—Gr. 4
Sadie Saulter School
Greenville, NC

Licensed to Learn

Looking for an alternative to posting a class list on your door on the first day of school? Using a computer, design for each student a license plate that shows his name, your name, the school name, and the month and year. Glue each license plate on colored construction paper; then laminate the plates and secure them to the classroom door. After the first month of school, let students tape the plates to their desks or hang them in their rooms at home.

Gary L. Painter—Gr. 5
Springfield Elementary
Rileyville, VA

Vacation Posters

Give students a sneak peek into your social studies curriculum with this back-to-school activity! Check recent magazines for pages advertising free vacation information by mail. Request information on any vacation spots located within the states or countries that you will study this school year. Then, during the first week of school, have each student select one packet that you received. Have him look through his packet and design a poster describing an imaginary trip he took there over the summer. Provide time for students to share their posters with the class.

Colleen Proffitt—Gr. 5
Doe Elementary
Mountain City, TN

Happy Notes

At the beginning of the year, address two sets of postcards—one set addressed to individual parents and one set addressed to individual students. Every Thursday pull two students' postcards and their parents' postcards. Jot a quick, positive, and encouraging note about the student on each card. Put the cards in the mail by Friday so the students will receive them over the weekend. This only takes a couple of minutes and the results are terrific!

Nancy Oglevie—Gr. 5
Sheridan Elementary
Sheboygan, WI

HAPPY NOTE

Dear Mr. Mihans,
Richie has completed all of his work this week. He's a very hard worker!
Ms. Rogers

The Storage Desk

One obstacle to organization is a cluttered desk. But what does a student do when he has more supplies than storage space? Solve this problem by arranging student desks in groups of four. Place an extra empty desk at the end of each arrangement as shown. Encourage students to use this desk as an overflow area for supplies that don't fit in their own desks. Bye-bye, clutter!

Phyllis Ellett—Grs. 3–4 Multiage
Earl Hanson Elementary
Rock Island, IL

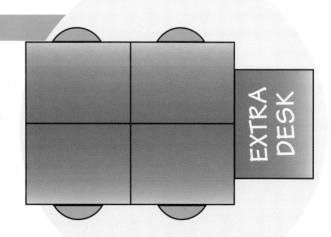

EXTRA DESK

Let your new students know they can bank on a great year! For each child, duplicate the bill pattern on page 17 on green paper. Cut out the center oval; then tape a photo of the new student behind it and post the finished product as shown. Add a border of pink paper piggy banks (pattern on page 17) on which students have written paragraphs describing their hopes for the school year or how they'd spend $1,000.

Karen Maresca—Gr. 6, St. Vincent de Paul School, Stirling, NJ

Post a lighthouse on a background of light and dark blue paper as shown. Add beams of light with yellow chalk. Have each student fold up and glue down the bottom inch or two of a white paper triangle. After labeling and coloring the boat's bottom as shown, have the student draw a vertical line on the sail and label it with words to describe himself. Have students use the words later in descriptive paragraphs about themselves.

adapted from an idea by Colleen Dabney, Williamsburg Christian Academy, Williamsburg, VA

We're a Perfect Mix!

Encourage class cooperation with this colorful display! On the first day of school, have each student finger-paint a few designs on a bulletin board backed with white paper. While the paint dries, have each student write a paragraph explaining what she can do to mix well with her classmates this year. Once the paint has dried, have each student sign her name on the board and share her paragraph. Post the paragraphs on the display.

Heather Graley, Columbus, OH

"In-vest" Some Time to Get Acquainted!

For a back-to-school display that doesn't require a big investment of time, copy the pattern on page 18 for each student. First, have the student decorate each pocket with the following: top left = favorite activity, top right = personal goal, bottom left = description of family, bottom right = favorite food. Then have him write his name on the label and color the vest with his favorite color or, to encourage reading, have students color their vests and post them on the board. Each time a child finishes a book, have him write the book's title and author on one of the pockets.

Kimberly A. Minafo, Carmel, NY

Take a giant step toward welcoming your new class with the fancy footwork of this display! On colorful paper, make a class supply of the sock pattern on page 19. Also make a class supply of the sneaker pattern on white paper. Glue a student's school picture on each sock. Then staple the socks to the display. On the first day, have each child decorate a sneaker pattern and then staple it atop her sock. It makes a "sock-sational" door display too!

J. Royce Brunk, Seoul Foreign School, Seoul, Korea

Show students they're in for a real treat this year with a fun back-to-school display! Write upcoming activities on self-sticking labels. Then place the labels on empty candy wrappers and bags. Staple the wrappers and bags on a bulletin board as shown. On the first day, discuss the activities with your new class. Then have each child trace his forearm and hand on colorful paper, cut out the tracing, label it with his name, and add it to the display. What a treat!

Therese Durhman—Gr. 5, Mountain View Elementary, Hickory, NC

Looking for a "tree-mendous" display for back-to-school? Post a large tree shape cut from butcher paper as shown. Give each student a cut-out paper apple to label with a few words of wisdom about how to succeed in school. After the child has glued green paper leaves to his apple, have him staple the cutout to the tree. Use the tree year-round by giving students a new set of seasonal cutouts and a new writing topic at the start of each month.

Kim Myers—Gr. 5
Albert Harris Elementary
Martinsville, VA

Lock up a sensational school year with this student-made display! Post a locker character like the one shown. Have each student fill in the rim of a lock pattern (page 20) with her own combination for unlocking a great year. Then have her label the lock with her name and lightly color it. It's all locked up!

Michelle Trubitz—Grs. 5–6, Brookside Upper Elementary, Westwood, NJ

Welcome students back with this "hot-doggity" door display! Post on your classroom door a character like the one shown. On the first day of school, have each student label a hot dog pattern (page 20) with his name; then have him decorate it using crayons and the key shown to indicate some of his favorite things. Post the hot dogs and a key on your door for a display that's frankly fantastic!

adapted from an idea by Donna DeRosa—Gr. 4
Good Shepherd Academy
Nutley, NJ

Frankly Speaking, I'm Glad You're Back!

Hayley
Emily
Carlos
Meredith
Ben
Steph
Jared
Reid
Jack
Molly

Condiments Key

Ketchup (red) = Reading
Mustard (yellow) = Sports
Relish (green) = Art
Chili (brown) = Math
Cheese (orange) = Computer
Onions (white) = Writing

SERVING ROOM 213

Tia — Messenger
Chris — Supplies
Nick — Computer
Min — Clock
Caleb — Plants
Ashley — Library
Bryce — Chalkboard
Sara — P.E.
Trish — Art
SERVERS

Assign classroom jobs in a jiffy with this display. Cover a board with a vinyl tablecloth. Add napkins and paper plates labeled with your classroom jobs as shown. Also label an index card for each student. To assign a job, pin a student's card to a plate. Store unused cards in a paper plate pocket stapled to the board as shown.

Donna G. Pawloski—Gr. 4, Primos Elementary, Primos, PA

This back-to-school display is sure to set the "moooood" for a great year! Enlarge the cow pattern on page 21 to use as a centerpiece for the board. Make a supply of the same pattern to attach to the board around the centerpiece. For a welcome-to-our-school display, write a staff member's name on each pattern. As a classroom display, write a student's name on each copy of the pattern. Tie a real cowbell around the large cow's neck just for fun!

Kerry Gray and Cathy Rozzi, St. Francis Xavier School, Acushnet, MA

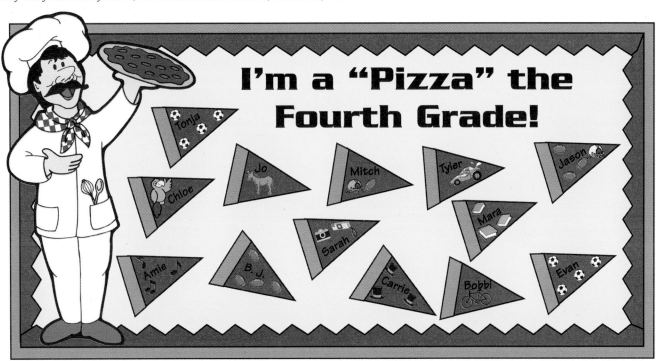

No matter how you slice it, this student-created bulletin board will be a hit! First, enlarge and color the chef pattern on page 21. Next, provide each student with a wedge-shaped sheet of art paper. Instruct each student to write her name on the wedge in large black letters and then add small symbols on the wedge as pizza ingredients. These symbols should represent interests of the student: hobbies, sports, favorite books, etc. Have each student outline her ingredients with a black marker and then color her pizza slice bright red.

Perry Stio—Gr. 4, M. L. King School, Piscataway, NJ

Kaley

Stephen

A "Scooper-Duper" Class

Here's a sweet idea for a back-to-school bulletin board! Use a knife to carefully cut ice-cream cones in half. Write each student's name on a cone half with a marker; then use rubber cement to attach the cones to the board. Next, rubber-cement polyester fiberfil above each cone to resemble ice cream. To finish, sprinkle glitter on each cone filling. Title the board "[Teacher's name]'s 'Scooper-Duper' Class!"

Cathy Butler
Shawnee Maplewood School
Lima, OH

Guessing-Game Bulletin Board

Arm yourself with a camera to produce a winning bulletin board that helps students get to know their classmates. Take a snapshot of each child during the first week of school; then have him copy and complete the information shown on an index card. Mount each photo and its card on a bulletin board titled "Who Am I?" Next, staple a paper flap over each snapshot to conceal it. No student will be able to resist reading the clues, taking a guess, and lifting the flap to see if his guess is right!

Lisa Waller Rogers
Austin, TX

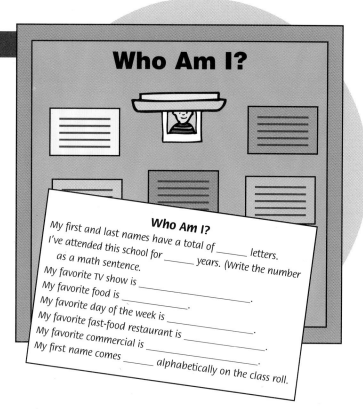

Who Am I?

Who Am I?
My first and last names have a total of _____ letters.
I've attended this school for _____ years. (Write the number as a math sentence.
My favorite TV show is _____
My favorite food is _____.
My favorite day of the week is _____
My favorite fast-food restaurant is _____.
My favorite commercial is _____.
My first name comes _____ alphabetically on the class roll.

YOU CAN DO IT!

Anything's possible!

Star Light, Star Bright!

Brighten up the classroom for your new students with this star-studded bulletin board idea. First, cover a bulletin board with black garbage bags. Then cut out star shapes from neon paper and label them with positive phrases as shown. Title the display "Star Light, Star Bright, Let's Start the Year Off Right!"

Kathy Wolford
Galion, OH

Dazzling Displays

Looking for a neat way to spruce up your bulletin boards? Buy plastic party tablecloths and matching paper plates that relate to themes you teach or topics kids love. For example, a black-and-white-checkered plastic tablecloth with matching racing plates makes a dazzling "Race Into Reading!" display. Look for great bargains at closeout sales, especially after holidays.

Pam Rawls—Gr. 4
Harpeth Valley Elementary
Nashville, TN

I've been looking forward to school because I get to see my friends!

Swimming Back to School

Make a splash with this eye-catching back-to-school bulletin board! Cover a board with various shades of blue paper cut into waves. Title the display "It's Time to Get Back in the Swim of Things." Next, duplicate a simple fish pattern for each student. Write the following sentence starter on the board: "I've been looking forward to school because…" Give each student a fish pattern when she arrives on the first day of school. Have her copy the sentence starter onto her fish and complete it by adding the best thing about returning to school. After the student decorates her fish, have her add it to the bulletin board.

Julia Alarie
Essex Middle School
Essex, VT

We're All Connected!

Use this creative bulletin board idea to post your students' names at the beginning of the year. Write each student's name in large print on an enlarged piece of grid paper; then cut out the name. Arrange the names to look like a crossword puzzle on a bulletin board titled "We're All Connected!"

Randee Bonagura
Fairfield Elementary
Massapequa, NY

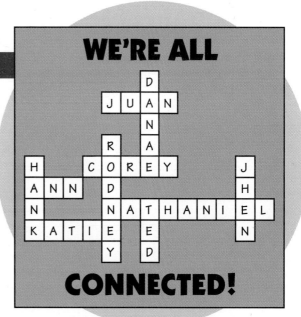

In this room, it's okay to make mistakes!

A Banner Idea

Add color to your classroom and create a feel-good atmosphere with this banner idea! Use die-cut letters to spell an inspirational quote. Glue the letters to a long strip of bulletin board paper. Then laminate the banner and hang it on a wall or from the ceiling. You can't beat these colorful, inspirational, and cheap space fillers!

Heather Eubank—Gr. 5
Willow Brook Elementary
Creve Coeur, MO

You've Got to Be Kidding!

Welcome your new students to your classroom with this rib-tickling display. Visit your school media center to find a book of children's jokes and riddles. Type several jokes that contain names, replacing the original names with those of your students. Print the jokes on different colors of bright paper and post them on a bulletin board titled "You've Got to Be Kidding!" Students will love being the stars of this back-to-school display—no kidding!

Teresa Munson
Warsaw, MO

Joseph: I tried to call the zoo but couldn't get through.
Brandon: Why?
Joseph: The lion's busy.

Back-to-School Bulletin Board

Need a quick, easy, and colorful back-to-school bulletin board? Get a piece of bulletin board paper big enough to cover the board. Lay the paper on the floor. Using bright primary colors of paint, have each student make a handprint on the paper. Write the name of the student below his handprint. After the paint has dried, have each student write two facts about himself inside his handprint. Finally, staple the paper to the bulletin board. Students and parents will enjoy reading everyone's "hand-y" work.

Janet Moody—Gr. 4
Truman Elementary
Lafayette, LA

Vest Pattern

Use with " 'In-vest' Some Time to Get Acquainted!" on page 9.

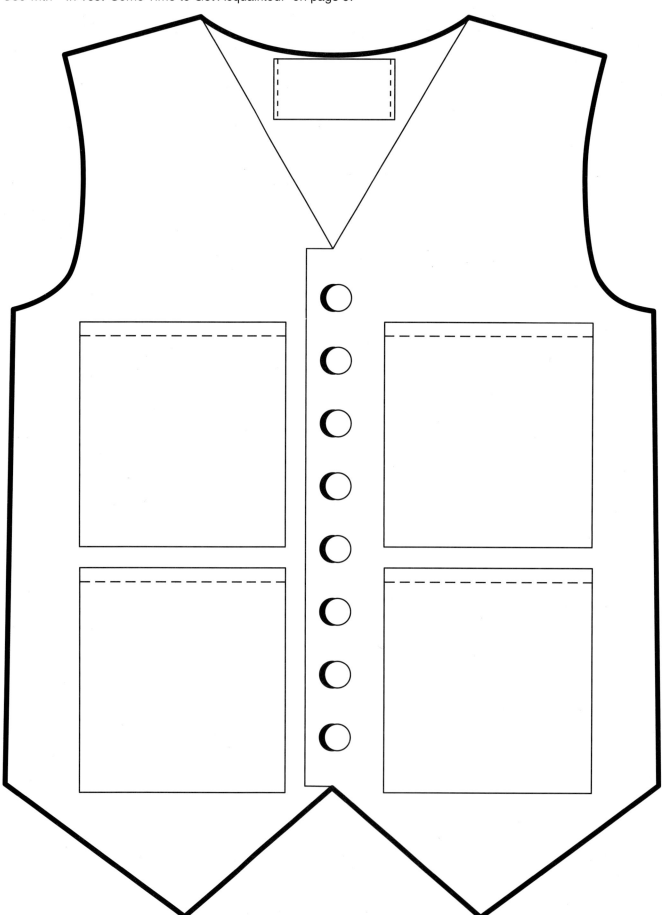

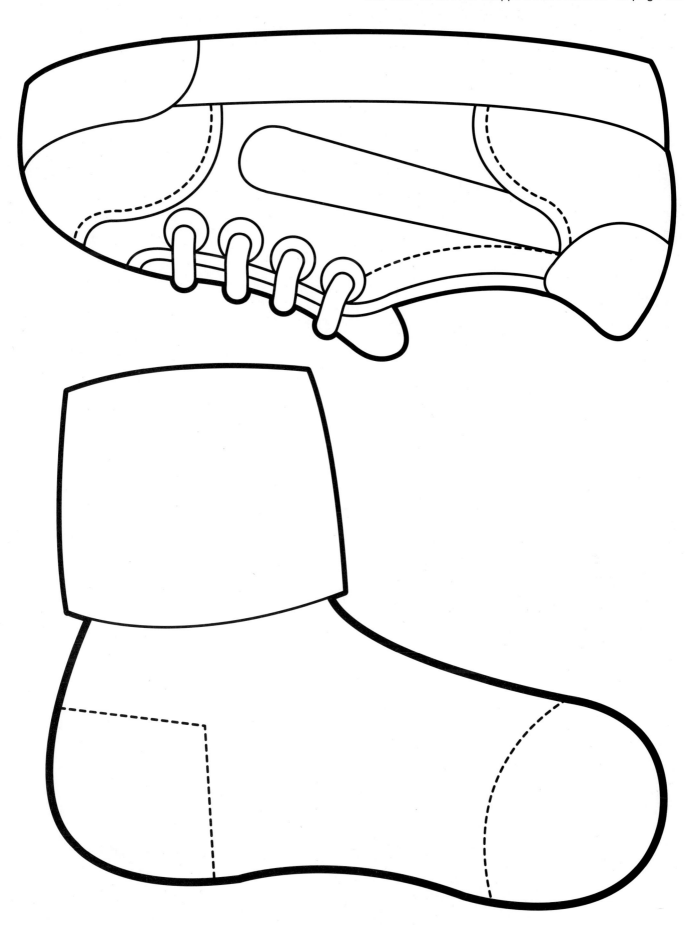

Lock Pattern
Use with "The Right Combination" on page 11.

Hot Dog Pattern
Use with "Frankly Speaking, I'm Glad You're Back!" on page 12.

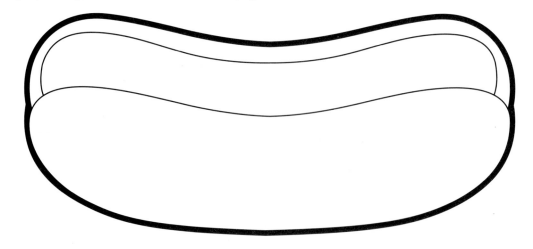

Cow Pattern

Use with "'Mooo-ving' Into a New School Year!" on page 13.

Chef Pattern

Use with "I'm a 'Pizza' the Fourth Grade!" on page 13.

Homeward-Bound Mail

Homeward-Bound Mail

Recycle an old mailbox from home by giving it a new use at school. First, give the mailbox a fresh coat of paint. Assign one student to be the class mailperson for a week. When you receive notices that need to go home at the end of the day, immediately place them inside the mailbox and put the flag up. Explain to your mailperson that when the flag is up, he has notes to pass out to class members at the end of the day. Never again will you find buried notes on your desk that should've gone home with students!

Michelle Kasmiske
Monroe Elementary
Janesville, WI

Simple Storage for Seasonal Essentials

Organize those monthly and seasonal bulletin boards and activities with these sturdy pockets. Stack two sheets of poster board and staple together all but the top sides to create a large pocket. Label the contents on the outside of the pocket. For smaller items and monthly masters or handouts, staple the sides of a legal-size manila folder, leaving the top open. Store the smaller folders in the larger monthly pockets. Place all the items together in a sturdy box that's been decorated by your students.

Theresa Azzolino—Gr. 6
Washington School
Lodi, NJ

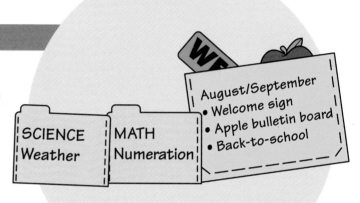

SCIENCE
Weather

MATH
Numeration

August/September
• Welcome sign
• Apple bulletin board
• Back-to-school

Bulletin Board Letters File

Organize your bulletin board letters with this easy idea. Obtain a file or large recipe box with alphabetical dividers. Put all the *A*s behind the *A* divider, the *B*s behind the *B* divider, and so on. Your letters will be right at your fingertips and easy to find when you need them!

Patty J. Vermeer—Gr. 4
Galva-Holstein Elementary
Holstein, IA

Cooking Cart

Make cooking in the classroom as easy as pie by pooling your faculty's cooking tools. First, ask all teachers who cook in their classrooms to donate any utensils to a school cooking cart. Collect and store the assorted utensils in bins on a portable cart. When a teacher cooks in her classroom, she can simply wheel in the cooking cart. Talk about meals on wheels!

Kim Helgeson—Gr. 5
Pecatonica Elementary
Hollandale, WI

Keeping Track of Books

Try this simple way of keeping track of textbooks or dictionaries. First, line up the books in the order that you wish. Then attach a strip of colored tape diagonally from the top corner of the first book to the bottom corner of the last book. Use scissors to snip between each book; then press down the edges of the tape. At a glance you can see if a book is missing.

Debbie Moreno—Gr. 5
Santa Fe Intermediate School
League City, TX

Cereal-Box Homework Caddies

Having a place to deposit assignments can really help disorganized students stay on top of their work. Have each student bring an empty cereal box to school. Help students cut their boxes as shown; then provide glue and colorful paper so students can cover the boxes. Assign each child a number to write on the front of her box. Then staple the boxes together side by side. Each morning have students deposit homework assignments in their cereal-box cubbies. As you check the boxes each morning, you'll notice in a snap who's come to school unprepared!

Jennifer Kendt—Grs. 4–5
Ohio School
North Tonawanda, NY

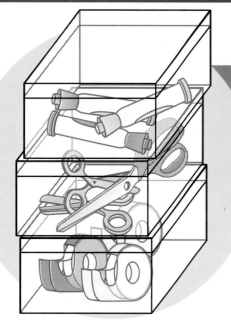

Crystal-Clear Storage

Avoid spending your valuable teaching time searching for frequently used supplies with the help of this practical suggestion. Store all of your small supplies—such as tape, scissors, and markers—in clear, plastic shoeboxes. Stack the boxes on top of one another in a convenient location in your classroom. How's that for an easy way to save time and stay organized?

Sharon Abell
Mineral Springs Middle School
Winston-Salem, NC

Photo Album Filing

Keep track of those great unit ideas you've copied or photos of favorite bulletin boards with this organizational tip. Purchase a photo album that has magnetic pages. Then just slip your ideas and photos under the clear covers of the pages. If desired, remove the pages from the album and arrange them in a binder with labeled dividers. These pages are also perfect for safeguarding receipts you'll need at tax preparation time.

Sara R. Grissom—Gr. 5
Atlantis Elementary
Cocoa, FL

Right angle

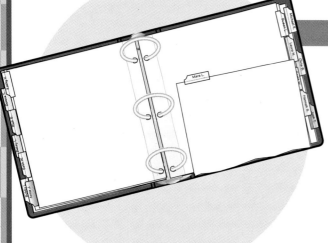

Information Superbook

Keep all of your students' vital information in one place with this supersimple idea. Purchase a large three-ring binder and add a tabbed divider for each student. Store important information in the notebook for each child, such as goals determined by parents, the student, and the teacher; work samples for each grading period; individualized education plans; concerns that a parent or a student has that you need to be aware of; reading records; assessments; and parent communications. Remove and send home items periodically, or keep everything until the end of the year. Either way, you'll have a handy, organized record of each student's progress and parent communications.

Donna Viola—Grs. 4–5
Roosevelt Elementary
McPherson, KS

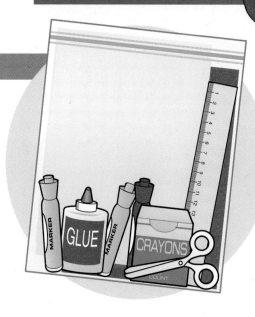

Take-Home Project Kits

With these kits, you can be sure that all students have access to the supplies they need for homework projects. To make a kit, fill a large plastic storage bag with basic supplies, such as markers, glue, a ruler, a pair of scissors, a box of crayons, and several sheets of 9" x 12" construction paper. Make about five or six kits available for students to check out for two to three days at a time. Now every child will have the tools she needs to create a great project!

Lisa Staub
Columbia, MD

A Pocketful of Organization

Are you constantly searching for the small pieces that accompany bulletin board sets? Attach a Press-on Pocket to the back of the largest character in each set. Store the small pieces for the set in the pocket along with the letters for the bulletin board caption. The next time you get ready to put up that bulletin board, all the pieces you need will be right at your fingertips!

Teena Anderson—Grs. K–6
Wayne County District 25
Pender, NE

First-Day Folders

Need an effective system for organizing the mountain of papers that are sent home the first day of school? Purchase one pocket folder for each child and write his name on the front. Place papers that don't need to be returned in the left-hand pocket. Place papers that need to be filled out and returned in the right-hand pocket. (Make a few extra folders for new students who arrive later in the school year.) Have students return the folders the next day with the completed paperwork inside. Simply pull and sort the forms from each returned folder. Then use the emptied folders as portfolios, for storing computer lab work, or as homework folders.

Nancy Curl—Gr. 6
Olson Middle School
Tabernacle, NJ

Allison Harvey

Star Student

Monthly Portfolio Envelopes

Seal up a month's supply of student work with this simple idea. At the beginning of the month, provide each student with a large manila envelope and a sheet of paper from a themed or seasonal notepad. Have each student glue the sheet to the outside of her envelope; then have her decorate her envelope with drawings or stickers. Have the student keep creative work, graded tests, and photographs of special projects inside the envelope. At the end of the month, have her select the work she wants to include in her portfolio and take home the rest. Then give her a new envelope and sheet of holiday notepaper for the upcoming month. Not only does this eliminate papers stuffed in the student's desk, but it also gives her the opportunity to review her work with her parents.

Joyce Hovanec—Gr. 4
Glassport Elementary
Glassport, PA

Color-Coded Notebooks

Have you ever discovered a student's math work in his reading journal? Or his journal writing in his learning log? To help students readily recognize and use the appropriate spiral notebook, try this color-coded tab system. Laminate several sheets of construction paper, one color for each subject-area notebook that your students use. Cut the sheets into 1½" x 9" strips and give each student one strip of each color. Direct the student to tape each strip to the inside cover of the corresponding notebook, leaving about one inch extending above the top. Then, at the front of the classroom, post large paper strips in the same colors labeled with the matching subjects. When it's time to use a notebook, students can easily identify the right one!

Julie VandeBerg—Gr. 4
Rosendale Intermediate School
Brandon, WI

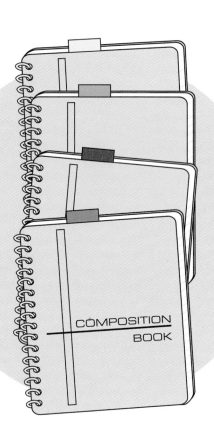

COMPOSITION BOOK

All-in-One Binder

Use a three-ring binder to keep your teacher essentials all in one place. Make a lesson-plan template that includes your lunchtime, special times, and other weekly scheduled activities. Make several copies of the template; then place them in a three-ring binder with your gradebook, stickers, grading scale, and other important information. Everything you need will be right at your fingertips!

Cathy Stemen
Cardington, OH

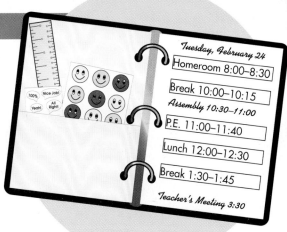

Classroom Library Organization

Looking for an easy and practical way to organize your classroom library? Obtain several inexpensive dishpans. Then organize your books either by genre (mysteries, nonfiction, etc.), topic (animals, friendship, etc.), or author, and place each set of books in a different labeled dishpan with this simple system. Students can get to the books easily and are therefore more motivated to read. When students look for a particular type of book or one written by a specific author, they can easily find what they're looking for!

Michelle Zakula—Gr. 5
St. Roman School
Milwaukee, WI

Organizing Scrap Paper

Don't waste your construction paper scraps; file them for easy student use. Position a large cardboard shoe organizer vertically. Fold various colors of large construction paper sheets in half to use as folders. Stand these colored folders in the slots of the organizer. Store your scraps of paper in the corresponding colored folders. Several folders can be stored in each slot, so there's plenty of room for all of your extra colors. Then when your students need construction paper for projects, they simply remove the desired colors from the folders and place the folders back in the organizer.

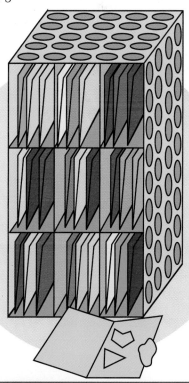

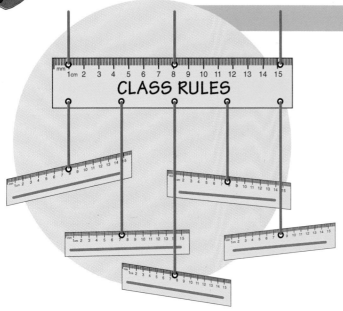

CLASS RULES

Classroom Rules Mobile

Let your students create an eye-catching classroom rules display. Begin by brainstorming a set of rules for the classroom with your students. Present a large poster board ruler labeled "CLASS RULES" along with several smaller poster board rulers. Draw names to see which students get to write the classroom rules on the small rulers. Attach each small ruler to the bottom edge of the large ruler using varying lengths of yarn; then suspend the large ruler from the ceiling.

Debbie Patrick
Park Forest Elementary
State College, PA

Classroom Promises

Do you involve students in developing your classroom rules? This year, try teaming up with your class to develop a set of student and teacher promises instead. Write the phrase "The students in [teacher's name]'s class promise to…" on a sheet of chart paper. Have students state helpful behaviors to finish the sentence. Then label another sheet of chart paper with "[Teacher's name] promises to…" and write your classroom responsibilities as the teacher. Type the completed lists into a single document and have each student sign one printed copy. Then give each student a copy and send another home to each family. What a great way to get your school year off to a positive start!

Kimberly A. Minafo—Gr. 4
Tooker Avenue Elementary
West Babylon, NY

Candy-Bar Class Rules

Misbehavior is no laughing matter. However, there's no harm in using some creative humor when introducing class rules. Post rules similar to the ones shown in your classroom, using real candy wrappers for key words. This colorful display encourages students to reread the rules and invites lighthearted laughs from visitors.

Diana Boykin
De Zavala Elementary
Midland, TX

There will be no Chuckles from the class when someone gives an unusual answer.

When a Dandy of an idea enters your mind, please raise your hand.

Mountains of compliments can't replace one insult. So please choose your words carefully.

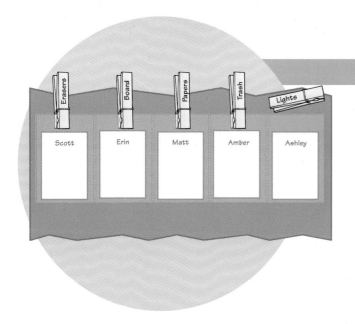

Looking for a quick way to assign classroom jobs each week? Then this tip's for you! Write each student's name on the top half of an index card. Slip one card in each pocket of a pocket chart as shown. Next, write each classroom job on a separate spring-type clothespin. Then clip one clothespin to the top of each pocket. To change the job assignments, simply move the clothespins one pocket to the right from one row to the next. When you reach the last pocket, just start over at the top!

Lynn Dunklee—Gr. 4
Danville School
Danville, VT

Classified Helpers

Create a new interest in classroom jobs by listing them in the classifieds! Cover a bulletin board with the classified section of a newspaper and title it "HELP WANTED!" Add two construction paper pockets—one labeled "For Hire" and the other "On Vacation"—to the display. Next, write each student's name on a different index card. Finally, fill the board's columns with the names and descriptions of different classroom jobs, leaving space beside each description to attach a library pocket.

Each Monday have a "manager" move the cards of students who had jobs last week into the "On Vacation" pocket. Then have her rotate the "For Hire" students' cards into the job pockets. Finally, have her move the "On Vacation" cards to the "For Hire" pocket.

Rami Parker—Gr. 4
Abita Springs Middle School
Abita Springs, LA

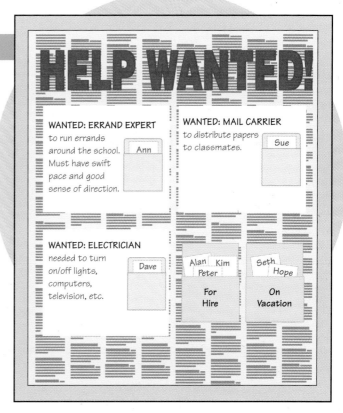

Weekly Jobs

- paper distributors
- paper collectors
- bookcase organizers
- shelf straighteners
- notice monitors—remind students to take weekly/daily notices home
- floor janitors
- classroom manager—do odd jobs for the teacher
- board cleaners
- desk straighteners
- center organizers
- sink cleaners
- paper and cupboard organizers
- job chart monitor—rotate names on job chart each week

Yearlong Jobs

- absentee monitors—record, collect, and explain missed assignments for absentees
- birthday monitor—keep track of student birthdays and oversee the signing of birthday cards
- library book monitor—check a list and remind students to return books
- homework board monitor—record assignments neatly on the board as they are given

Make your life easier and your classroom neater by recruiting students to perform both weekly and yearlong tasks. First, list all the tasks that must be done in your classroom on a regular basis. Divide the tasks into two categories: simple weekly jobs and those that a student could do with additional training. Then follow these simple steps:

- **Weekly Jobs:** Record the simple jobs on a weekly job chart. (See the sample for possible jobs.) Each week assign every child a task. If necessary, ask two students to share a job so that every child is employed.
- **Yearlong Tasks:** Consider recruiting students to perform certain jobs for the entire year. Think of tasks you do that a responsible child could be trained to tackle for you (see the list shown). Before hiring anyone for these positions of honor, observe students to identify who might make the most qualified employees. Then train the recruits accordingly. If desired, "pay" your yearlong helpers on the 15th and 30th of each month with extra-credit points so they'll learn some of the dynamics of a real-life working situation.

Lisa Boddez—Gr. 5
St. Mary's Elementary
Vancouver, British Columbia, Canada

Delicious Duties

Here's a sweet idea for a classroom job bulletin board! Cut out one Hershey's Kisses shape for each classroom job; then cover each cutout with aluminum foil. Write one classroom job on each cutout; then staple them onto a bulletin board titled "Delicious Duties." Label one slip of paper like the one found in Hershey's Kisses candy for each student. To assign a job to a student, simply pin the paper with his name to the top of the classroom job.

Lisa Lorincz—Gr. 5
Washington Elementary
Stevens Point, WI

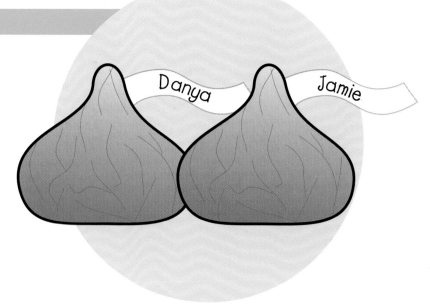

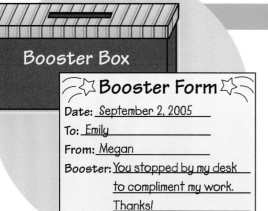

Booster Box

Booster Form

Date: September 2, 2005

To: Emily

From: Megan

Booster: You stopped by my desk to compliment my work. Thanks!

Booster Box

Create a positive classroom atmosphere with the following idea. Begin by explaining to students that a booster is an encouraging word or action. Make a supply of booster forms (see the illustration). Direct each student to fill out a booster form when a classmate has done a kind deed for her. Have the student place the completed form in the class booster box. Then, at the end of each week, draw one booster form from the box. Reward the two students mentioned on the form with a choice of class coupons, such as "Enjoy lunch made by the teacher" or "No homework tonight!" At the end of the grading period, have students place all of the booster forms in a booster book to share with parents on parent-teacher night.

Kimberly Marinelli—Gr. 5
La Barriere Crossings School
Winnipeg, Manitoba, Canada

Hugs, Hugs, and More Hugs!

Try this idea to encourage good behavior in your class. Divide students into groups of four and assign each group a numeral. Give each group a large coffee can covered with bright paper and labeled with the group's numeral. Then program small strips of colorful paper with the word *hugs*. Throughout the week, award each student who exhibits good behavior, such as whenever another adult compliments his behavior, whenever he is on task, or whenever he exhibits good behavior throughout the school, by dropping a hug into his group's can. On the following Monday, count the hugs; then reward students in the group that has collected the most hugs. Even though the hugs are paper, students will know that this is your way of letting them know how proud you are of their good behavior.

Sandy Carter—Gr. 5
Carpenter Elementary
Deer Park, TX

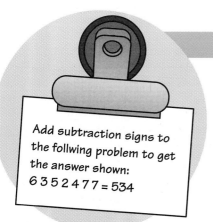

Add subtraction signs to the follwing problem to get the answer shown:
6 3 5 2 4 7 7 = 534

Daily Dynamos

Looking to keep your students busy in the morning before school begins? Start a collection of logic problems, trivia questions, and other brainteasers. Write each problem on a construction paper strip, using a different color of paper for each subject area. Each morning attach two or three problems to the chalkboard with magnetic clips. Direct each student to write the answers to the problems in a special notebook. Later in the day, review the answer to each problem.

Diane Moser—Gr. 5
Sangre Ridge Elementary
Stillwater, OK

Make Homework Count!	
Assignment	Date
1. Math, p.78	Oct. 5
2.	
3.	
4.	

Class Homework Motivator

Motivate students to be more consistent about turning in homework with an incentive that makes everyone a winner! Each time every student turns in an assignment on time, have one child record the assignment and date on a chart. (If a student is absent, give the class credit if he turns in the assignment the day he returns.) When the class has listed ten assignments, celebrate by letting students choose a special activity to enjoy later in the week.

Krystal Boxeth
Academia Cotopaxi
Quito, Ecuador

The Party Tree

To get the year off to a good start, display a Party Tree on a bulletin board. Make construction paper leaves and program each one with a compliment similar to the ones shown. Have the student leader for the day take one leaf to the teacher of each special class (art, music, etc.) that students attend during the day. That teacher sends the leaf back to you if the entire class has shown appropriate behavior during her time. When the Party Tree is filled with a predetermined number of leaves, the reward is, of course, a party!

Susan Bell—Gr. 5
Lincoln Elementary
St. Charles, MO

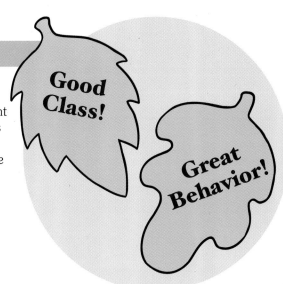

Good Class!

Great Behavior!

Name _____

Congratulations!

Because you have worked hard, you will be given free answers to ten homework questions of your choice!

Directions: When you wish to receive a free answer, give this paper to your teacher. She will mark your paper and subtract one box below. You may use no more than two on an assignment. Use them wisely! When they're gone, they're gone!

1	2	3	4	5	6	7	8	9	10

Ten Free Answers

Reward students who consistently turn in homework by giving them a much deserved break. Create a sheet similar to the one shown which features a cute cartoon or clip-art character. At the end of each grading period, present a copy of the sheet to each student who completed every assignment during that period. When a student wants to skip a question on an assignment, have her bring her reward sheet and assignment to you. Write "okay" next to the question on her assignment; then mark out one numbered box on the student's reward sheet. Specify that a student not skip more than two questions on any one assignment. Also reserve the right to refuse the use of the sheet on questions you want all students to answer. In time, more and more students will scramble to turn in all of their work and earn a sheet of free answers!

Sharon Vance—Gr. 5
Nash Intermediate School
Kaufman, TX

bookshelves

Easy-to-Spot Reminders

Do you have students who sometimes forget to do their assigned classroom jobs? Solve that problem by using simple visual reminders! Attach a magnetic clip to each student's desk. Also write each classroom job on a separate index card. When a student is assigned a new job, have her clip that card on her desk. One quick glance reminds her that she's got a job to do!

Joyce Hovanec—Gr. 4
Glassport Elementary
Glassport, PA

Computer Guidelines

Start the year with this handy computer station tip. Post a step-by-step chart near the computer after instructing students on computer routines, such as loading and removing diskettes, turning on and shutting down the system, and using the printer. With the basics outlined and at your students' fingertips, you can focus your attention on more complicated computer instruction.

Julie Granchelli
Lockport, NY

First-of-the-Year Contracts

Start the year on a positive note by providing each student with a copy of an "I Plan to Do My Best This Year" contract. (See the illustration.) Discuss ways that students can do their best throughout the year. Then direct each student to sign and date his contract and place it in the front of his notebook. Encourage each student to look back at his contract whenever he needs a dose of inspiration!

Chana Rochel Zucker—Gr. 5
Be'er Hagolah Institute
Brooklyn, NY

I Plan to Do My Best This Year!

If I think I can, I will!

_____
signed

_____
date

Issued by
Ms. Zucker   Grade 5

"Day-o-meter" Monitor

Use a simple visual reminder to motivate students to stay on task and be on their best behavior. Just write the numbers 1 to 10 vertically on a magnetic board, with 10 at the top. Place a fun magnet next to the number that indicates the class's behavior (10 being best). Then move the magnet up or down throughout the day to let students know at a glance how their behavior rates.

Leighton Rudd—Gr. 4
Bucklin Grade School
Bucklin, KS

Daily Index Cards

To help you keep track of daily events, absentees, and discipline issues, use a spiral-bound set of index cards. Write the date at the top of a card. Then list on the card any changes in daily plans, absent students, classwork and homework assignments, or problems that arise during the day. You can easily flip back to earlier dates to check work accomplished or to see when students were absent.

Hope Miller—Gr. 6
Willard Middle School
Willard, OH

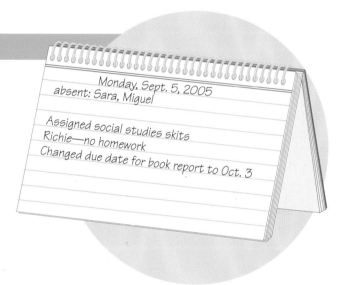

No-Fuss Lunch Count

Make taking the daily lunch count and attendance a picnic! Hot-glue two labeled wicker paper-plate holders to a piece of decorated cardboard as shown. Next, attach clothespins—each labeled with a different student's name—along the top of the board. Finally, title the board "Lunch Count" and attach it to a wall or bulletin board. As each student arrives at school, have him clip his clothespin to the appropriate plate. The clips that remain on the top of the board identify those students who are absent.

Brenda Fendley—Gr. 4
Blossom Elementary
Blossom, TX

Charting Absent Students

September						
Sun	Mon	Tue	Wed	Thu	Fri	Sat
				1	2 ~~Alex~~	3
4	5 ~~Nick~~	6 Amy	7	8 Jamal	9 Alex	10
11	12	13	14	15	16	17
18	19	20	21	22	23	24
25	26	27	28	29	30	

Use a large desk calendar to chart absentees, parent notes, and missed assignments. Each morning write the names of absent students in that day's calendar box. At a glance, you can note any patterns of absenteeism, such as a child missing too many Fridays. Whenever you get a note from a parent regarding an absence, simply mark through that child's name on the calendar and file the note. To keep track of make-up work, circle the child's name when her assignments are completed. In a snap, you can see any info you need about an absent student.

Sharon Zacharda—Gr. 4
West View Elementary
Pittsburgh, PA

Craft Stick Names

At the beginning of the year, program a craft stick with each student's name; then store the sticks in a plastic utensil tray to use every day, all year long! Use the sticks to call on students during class discussions or choose a stick and ask that student to summarize a previous child's remarks. You can also use the sticks to choose students to perform special tasks, determine the order of student presentations, and make classroom seating charts.

Carla Martin—Grs. 4–5
Purdy Elementary
Gig Harbor, WA

Made in the Shade!

Here's a bright idea for this year's hall passes. Take advantage of summer sales by purchasing two pairs of inexpensive sunglasses. Write "Pass" and your name on the earpieces of each pair. Students will enjoy wearing these cool shades as they perform duties that require traveling from the classroom and back.

Stella Bizzio—Gr. 5
LeRosen Elementary
Lafayette, LA

Hot Diggity Dog— A New Year!

Back-to-School Ideas for Busy Teachers

Hot diggity dog—a new year is here! Add a spot of fun to the first days with the following creative back-to-school activities and reproducibles. Our bet is you'll soon be spotted with a class full of enthusiastic, eager-to-learn students!

First-Day Doggie Bags

Calm first-day jitters and involve early arrivals in productive activities with the help of—you guessed it—doggie bags! Add student instructions and your signature to the doggie bag pattern on page 39 before duplicating it on red construction paper for each child. Cut out each pattern and label the collar with a student's name; then cut small slits along the dotted lines of the dog's mouth and insert a new pencil as shown. Glue the pattern to a small white paper bag (look for ones with handles) that you have decorated with black spots. Fill the bag with items such as the interest inventory on page 41 (used in the following bulletin board activity), a copy of the reproducible filmstrip activity on page 42, a copy of your class schedule, and other important first-day items. Place the bags on the students' desks before children begin arriving. It won't be hard to spot the quick smiles from students as they dig into their doggie bags!

LOOK WHO'S BEEN **SPOTTED** IN MY CLASS!

Look Who's Been Spotted in My Class!

Welcome students back to school with a bulletin board that's a cinch to spot! Enlarge, color, and cut out the dalmatian pattern at the bottom of page 40; then mount it on a bulletin board as shown. Use white chalk or a white-leaded pencil to label the dog's spots with topics to be studied this year.

On the first day of school, give each student a copy of the interest inventory on page 41. Have students complete their inventories; then give each child a copy of the patterns at the top of page 40. After students cut out their patterns, have them tape or glue the pieces to the backs of their interest inventories as shown. After students have shared their inventories with the class, display the completed projects on the bulletin board. If desired, let students use markers to add spots to a plain white bulletin board border during their free time.

adapted from an idea by Vicki Bess—Gr. 6
Bracken County Middle School
Brooksville, KY

TRDavidson

I Was Really in a Spot When...

There's probably not anyone who hasn't been in a bit of a tight spot at least once! Discover the writing abilities of your new students by asking each one to write about a time when he was really in a spot. How did he get in such a predicament? How did he get out of it? What did he learn from the experience? What advice would he give someone who was in a similar sticky situation? If desired, create the first class book of the year by binding the stories together between construction paper covers that have been decorated with black spots.

How Many Toothpicks Can You Spot?

Introduce students to the scientific method with a back-to-school activity that's more than just a little fun! Begin by dividing students into four groups. Display four colors of toothpicks: blue, red, green, yellow. Then write on the board "Which toothpicks would be the easiest to spot if dropped in the grass?" Tell students that asking a question (or stating a purpose) is the first step in the scientific method. Next, have the class form a hypothesis to write on the board.

To test the hypothesis, assign a color to each group and have each group choose a leader. Try to schedule this step just before students leave for a special class. After students leave, scatter about 30 toothpicks of each color in a large grassy area of the playground as far from the school building as possible. When the class returns, give each leader a plastic bag. At your signal, each group works together to spot its colored toothpicks. What's the catch? Only the leader may pick up a toothpick; other group members must point to the found toothpicks and call out the name of the color. After this fun (and noisy) time is up, head back indoors to complete the last two steps of the scientific method. Have groups count their toothpicks and list the totals on the board; then work together to formulate a conclusion. Be prepared for a few surprises!

Betty Adams—Gr. 5, Staunton Elementary, Staunton, IN

Purpose
Hypothesis
Procedure
Observations
Conclus

How Many Mistakes Can You Spot?

Combine a getting-to-know-the-teacher activity with an introduction to proofreading skills. Before the first day of school, write a brief autobiography about yourself. Include information that kids love to find out about their teacher, such as your most embarrassing moment, your favorite subject, your favorite food, and the most exciting trip you ever took. Also include common proofreading errors in spelling, capitalization, and punctuation. Duplicate the finished autobiography and the proofreading checklist on page 42 for each student. Pair students and challenge them to use the checklist to see how many mistakes they can spot in your life story. Follow up this activity by having each child write a brief autobiography; then let partners use the checklist to proofread each other's papers. Have students staple the checklists inside their individual writing portfolios for future reference.

My Spot on the Team

During the first week of school, take individual photos of your students; then mount each photo in the center of a sheet of colorful paper. Have each student write a couple of phrases describing herself on her poster; then divide the class into teams and have each student use her poster to introduce herself to her teammates. Collect the posters and display them, by teams, on the walls of your classroom. At the end of the month, have each student write a compliment on the poster of each of her teammates. Assign new teams for the next month, rearranging the posters to display the new groupings. Continue the month-end compliment-writing session. By the end of the year, each of your students will have a poster that's packed with self-esteem boosters!

Susan B. Killian—Gr. 5
Pine Grove Elementary
Glen Arm, MD

Spot Art

Once cooperative teams are established, give them practice in working toward a common goal with a spot of art! Provide each team with a large piece of art paper, crayons or markers, glue, and an envelope containing several construction paper circles of various colors and sizes. Have each team glue its spots on the paper; then have teammates work together to incorporate the spots into a creative picture or scene. Post the pictures on a bulletin board along with the following poem:

Start with a few simple spots.
Then tell me what you see.
Isn't it just amazing
What those spots can be?

Where Were You Spotted This Summer?

Were you spotted on a sandy beach reading your favorite novel this summer? Or were you spotted hiking a nearby mountain? Summer vacations are as diverse as the students in your new class. And they provide the perfect opportunity for an exciting math group project. Follow these steps for a graphing activity that will leave your kids begging for more!

Steps:

1. As a class, discuss summer vacation questions to ask in your survey and talk about how to conduct the survey.
2. Decide on survey questions and procedures. Duplicate the survey for students to distribute to other classes.
3. Divide the class into teams (one team per grade level to be surveyed).
4. Have teams survey their assigned classrooms during the first week or two of school.
5. Review the types of graphs teams can make to display their information; then have each team choose a graph to make.
6. Have each team share its graph.
7. Combine the results; then decide as a class what type of graph to use to display schoolwide results.
8. Working in teams during free time, have students complete the schoolwide graph. Display the finished graph in a hallway, library, or cafeteria.

Susan Beresh—Grs. 4–5
Gibson School for the Gifted
Southfield, MI

The Literature Spot

With this fun dalmatians theme, you'll have the perfect lead-in to a literature unit on man's best friend. And there are plenty of wonderful children's books to get you started! Try the following titles:

Old Yeller by Fred Gipson

Where the Red Fern Grows by Wilson Rawls

Big Red by Jim Kjelgaard

A Dog on Barkham Street by Mary Stolz

Dominic by William Steig

The Incredible Journey by Sheila Burnford

Lassie Come Home
   by Eric Knight

Mishmash by Molly Cone

Sounder by William H. Armstrong

The Call of the Wild
   by Jack London

A Dog Called Kitty by Bill Wallace

Hurry Home, Candy
   by Meindert DeJong

Puppy Chow

After completing all of the sensational spot activities in this unit, your students are likely to come down with a bad case of spotted fever! The cure? How about an easy-to-make snack that packs a great energy punch? Fill individual resealable bags with the following yummy puppy chow. Place each bag inside a back-to-school doggie bag (see page 36). Or surprise students with the snack on the last day of your back-to-school unit. No matter when you serve it, you won't spot any leftovers!

Puppy Chow

¾ c. shelled sunflower seeds
¾ c. small walnut pieces
6 oz. package of chocolate chips
1 c. raisins or diced dried fruit
2 c. crunchy cold cereal (such as granola or oat bran)

Mix together in a large bowl. Pour half a cup of the mixture into each small bag.

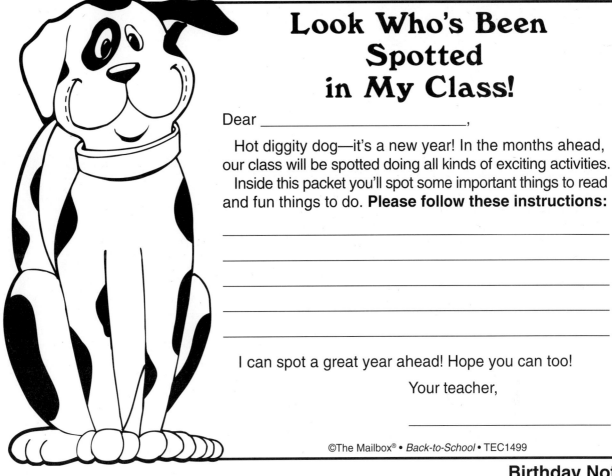

Look Who's Been Spotted in My Class!

Dear _____,

Hot diggity dog—it's a new year! In the months ahead, our class will be spotted doing all kinds of exciting activities. Inside this packet you'll spot some important things to read and fun things to do. **Please follow these instructions:**

_____

_____

_____

_____

_____

I can spot a great year ahead! Hope you can too!

Your teacher,

_____

©The Mailbox® • *Back-to-School* • TEC1499

Birthday Note

I Spot Someone With a Birthday!

Happy birthday, _____!

To help you "paws" and celebrate your big day, this card entitles you to skip homework tonight. Do I spot a smile?

ENJOY YOUR BIRTHDAY!

Signed: _____

Date: _____

©The Mailbox® • *Back-to-School* • TEC1499

Note to the teacher: Use the birthday note to celebrate students' birthdays. Recognize students with summer birthdays during the first or last month of school. *Adapted from an idea by Debi Montana—Gr. 6, M. L. Donovan School, Randolph, MA*

Dog Patterns

Use with "Look Who's Been Spotted in My Class!" on page 36.

Glue or tape to back of paper.

Glue or tape to back of paper.

The Spotlight's on You!

Fill in each spotlight. Draw a picture of yourself
in the blank spotlight at the top of the page.

Name a famous person with whom you'd love to be spotted.

What would someone spot you doing in your spare time?

Where might someone have spotted you this summer?

What kind of book are you likely to be spotted reading?

Which friend are you most likely to be spotted with?

What are two things you'll *never* be spotted doing in your spare time?

What school subject are you likely to be spotted doing well?

What are two strengths that are easy to spot in you?

What job would you like to be spotted doing when you're older?

What food would you most like to be spotted eating?

Would you rather be spotted working alone, with a partner, or in a group?

What spot in the world would you most like to visit?

What goal would you like to be spotted reaching this year?

Name a topic you'd like to be spotted studying this year.

Note to the teacher: Use with "First-Day Doggie Bags" and "Look Who's Been Spotted in My Class!" on page 36.

41

Name _____

Proofreading checklist

Time for a Spot Check!

Congratulations! As an author, you've just reached an important stage—editing. Read through your rough draft and mark the following checklist. Then go back and make any changes or corrections.

1. Did I indent each new paragraph? ☐

2. Does each sentence express a complete thought (no sentence fragments)? ☐

3. Are there any run-on sentences that need to be corrected? ☐

4. Do all of my sentences start the same way? (They shouldn't!) ☐

5. Did I capitalize correctly? ☐

6. Are there any misspelled words? ☐

7. Did I punctuate correctly? ☐

8. Are my sentences in the correct order? ☐

9. Did I include descriptive adjectives, adverbs, and verbs? If not, can I find better words to use? ☐

10. In each sentence, do the subject and verb agree? ☐

11. Did I tell who, what, where, when, and how? ☐

12. Does my written piece make sense? ☐

13. Did I leave out any words by mistake? ☐

14. Did I include my name in the piece? ☐

15. Is my work written or typed neatly? ☐

Note to the teacher: Use with "How Many Mistakes Can You Spot" on page 37.

Name _____

Making a filmstrip

The First Day on Film!

ACTION

Make a filmstrip of your first day at school. Draw a picture in each frame. In the numbered blanks, write a caption. Take the filmstrip and captions home to share with your family members!

1. _____

2. _____

3. _____

4. _____

5. _____

If you need more than one copy of this page, ask your teacher.

42

1 ◼ ◼ ◼ ◼ ◼
2 ◼ ◼ ◼ ◼ ◼
3 ◼ ◼ ◼ ◼ ◼
4 ◼ ◼ ◼ ◼ ◼
5 ◼ ◼ ◼ ◼ ◼

Note to the teacher: Use with "First-Day Doggie Bags" on page 36.

Got a Spot of Free Time?

Monday	Tuesday	Wednesday	Thursday	Friday
Would you wear a *homburg* or eat it? Use a dictionary to find out.	Vowels are worth 53 cents each. Consonants are worth 27 cents. How much is your full name worth? Use a calculator to find out.	A *pangram* is a sentence that includes all the letters of the alphabet. Write a pangram. Remember that it must make sense!	"All that glitters is not gold." What do you think this proverb means? Write your answer.	Write five clues about any state. Give the clues to a friend to guess the state.
List seven favorite foods, seven favorite animals, and seven good things about you.	Draw a picture for a child to color. Write a one-sentence caption under the picture.	How many toes are in your class? Multiply to find out.	Write the names of ten countries that are not in North America. Be sure the spelling is correct.	You must teach a space alien ten sentences he/she will need to know to make it through the first day on Earth. Write the sentences.
Make a list of at least 20 words that have to do with peace.	What would you do if you were awakened at your school desk and were told that you had been asleep for four weeks? Write your answer in a paragraph.	Write three questions you would like to find answers for next week.	Find out each of your classmates' favorite season of the year. Make a graph or chart to show your survey results. Autumn Winter Spring Summer	List eight ways to cook without using electricity.
"A page is to a book as a piece is to a puzzle." Write five other analogies.	How many words can you write that contain the letter sequence *ach*? Here are two to get you started: *beach, ache.* ACH	Estimate how many paper clips are needed to go across your desk; then measure for yourself.	Name as many things as possible that scratch.	Write a task to put on the next free-time calendar!

Note to the teacher: Have each student staple this page in a file folder. Completed work can be stored inside the folder.

A "Fin-tastic" First Day

Our Readers' Favorite Activities for the First Day of School

Fishin' around for some new ways to make the first day of school extra special? With the following "fin-tastic" ideas from our readers, your kids will be back in the swim of things in no time!

First-Day Envelopes

Keep kids busy on the first morning of school with this easy idea. Use colorful stickers to decorate a large manila envelope (or a lunch-size paper bag) for each child. Stuff the envelopes with the items shown and place them on students' desktops. Not only can the activities buy you time for completing first-day tasks, but students can use the envelopes at the end of the day to take home important forms and information.

Garlene Turner
Mildred Dean Elementary
Butler, KY

- a back-to-school puzzle
- a new, sharpened pencil
- a box of crayons
- an interesting picture to color
- a welcome letter from you (Make a note in your plan book for the last week of school to have this year's students write the letters for next year's class.)
- a nutritious snack, such as a box of raisins or a bag of trail mix

Me Boxes

Find out all about your new students with this first-day homework assignment. One week before school begins, send each child a note welcoming him to your class. In the note, ask him to decorate the outside of a shoebox with words or pictures that represent his personal qualities, the things he values, and the people he loves. Inside the box, have him place three items that are special to him. Then, on the first day of school, divide students into groups to share their boxes with one another.

Shawn L. Parkhurst
Canadian Academy
Kobe, Japan

Getting-Acquainted Letters

It's a familiar first-day dilemma: parents who arrive with their kids want to chat with you, but students are also waiting at their desks for something to do. Say so long to such a scenario with this getting-acquainted activity! First, write a three-paragraph letter about yourself to place on each student's desk along with a sheet of colorful stationery and a new pencil. In the first paragraph of the letter, tell about your family and hobbies. In the second paragraph, share what you did during the summer. In the third paragraph, state your goals for the year. Conclude the letter by asking each student to answer it (in the same three-paragraph format) using the stationery and new pencil.

Shawn L. Parkhurst

I am a boy with light brown hair and brown eyes who likes to ride horses. I love pepperoni pizza, strawberry ice cream, and the chocolate chip cookies that my mom makes. I have a dog named Checkers and a cat named Claws.

Guess Who!

Help students take a closer look at their new classmates with this first-day writing activity. Review the qualities of good descriptive writing. Then have each student cut out a copy of the pattern on page 49. Direct the child to write a description of himself on the pattern (without including his name); then have him write his name on the back. Arrange the magnifying glasses and a copy of your class roster on a bulletin board titled "Can You Guess Who's in [name of teacher]'s Class?" During free time, have students try to match the names and descriptions. On back-to-school night, challenge each parent to guess which magnifying glass describes her child!

Michelle Trubitz—Grs. 5–6
Brookside Upper Elementary
Westwood, NJ

Big Rules

Make expectations crystal clear on the first day with this surefire activity. In advance, write each of your class rules on a different sheet of poster board. (Keep the list to three to five general rules; see the sample list below.) On the first day, ask each student to list on index cards rules that she thinks are important (one per card). Next, introduce your rules by displaying the posters. In turn, have each child read one of her rules aloud. Discuss with students how the rule fits under one of your general rules. Then have that student tape her card to the appropriate poster. After all the cards have been shared, divide students into groups and assign each group a different general rule. Each group's job is to design a poster that shows how the student cards explain the assigned rule more clearly. Display the students' posters next to yours. Then, when disciplining a child later in the year, point to the posters as a reminder of the rules that everyone agreed on.

Teena Andersen—Grs. 4–6, Hadar Public School
Pilger, NE

Sample Rules
- Treat others with kindness.
- Always do your best work.
- Be a responsible member of this class.

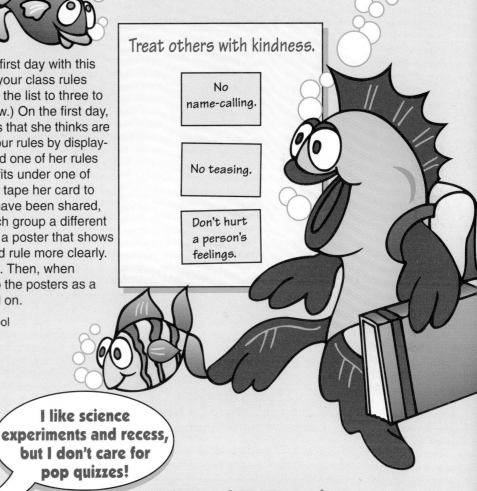

Treat others with kindness.

No name-calling.

No teasing.

Don't hurt a person's feelings.

I like science experiments and recess, but I don't care for pop quizzes!

Pam Crane

A Few of My Favorite (and Least Favorite) Things

Share your expectations for the school year with this fun brainstorming activity. First, have students brainstorm a list of the things they like best about school: activities they enjoy, topics they like learning about, kinds of tests they prefer, etc. Next, ask students to name things that they don't like. After this list is complete, turn the tables by sharing *your* favorite things, such as students who raise their hands before speaking and kind attitudes toward others. Also share your least favorite things, such as impolite or disruptive behavior. Suggest that you'll try to avoid the things students dislike if they'll avoid yours. Then make a pact, agreeing to make this a pleasant year for everyone!

Jaimie K. Hudson, Pace, FL

45

Classmate Crossword

Help students learn how to spell one another's names correctly with this fun first-day activity. First, let each child have the fun of writing his name on the chalkboard. Then give each student a sheet of half-inch graph paper on which to create a crossword puzzle that includes all of his classmates' names. Now that spells *fun!*

Jennifer Balogh-Joiner—Gr. 4
Franklin Elementary, Franklin, NJ

Charming Groups

Hearts	Stars
Richie	Cameron
Mary	Rose
Clevell	Logan
Lisa	Courteney
Ji-Hae	Matt

Rainbows	Moons
Hannah	Meredith
Kenzie	Casey
Jack	Abby
Amanda	Michael
Stacey	Devin

Charmed, I'm Sure!

Give your lucky students a charming first day with this nifty activity! In advance, purchase a box of Lucky Charms cereal. Fill a plastic cup with one marshmallow cereal piece for each student so that you end up with several same-size groups (for example, five hearts, five stars, five rainbows, and five moons). Keep the rest of the cereal for later. Also, cut a horseshoe shape from paper for each student and label it with her name. Display the cutouts on a bulletin board titled "[Name of teacher]'s Lucky Charms."

On the first day of school, greet each child at the door by saying you are charmed to meet her. Then ask her to pick a piece of cereal from your cup and keep it at her desk. Explain to students that the shapes they chose represent their assigned cooperative groups. Have each child write her name on a poster labeled with the marshmallow types. Then direct students' attention to the bulletin board. Discuss how students can make good luck happen by developing positive work habits and behavior. Then bring out plastic cups, plastic spoons, and milk to eat the remaining cereal together!

Kimberly Minafo—Gr. 4, Tooker Avenue Elementary
West Babylon, NY

My Very Own Holiday

Get ready for some never-before-celebrated holidays—and increased self-esteem—with this creative first-day activity. Have each child choose a different date on the calendar as his own special holiday. Direct the student to write a paragraph that not only names the holiday and explains its rationale but includes two ways the class can celebrate it. Then mark that day on the class calendar. As each holiday arrives, allow the appropriate child to announce it to the class and explain how it will be celebrated. Let the celebrating begin!

Sr. Ann Claire Rhoads, St. Ann Catholic School
Fayetteville, NC

October 3

CHERRY DAY!

—Have cherries for a snack.
—Write tall tales that have cherry-character heroes.

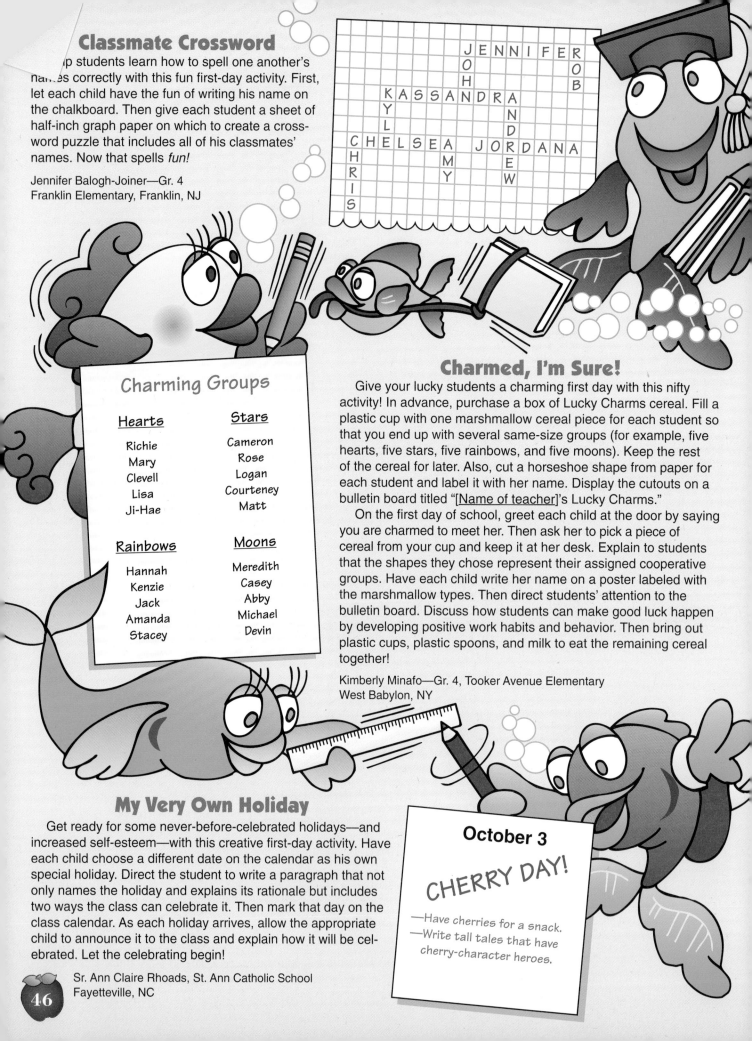

A Sweet Way of Getting to Know You

Treat students to a sweet way of getting to know one another with this activity. Give each child a small bag of M&M's or Skittles candy. Direct him to reach into his bag without looking and remove one piece of candy. Have students holding the same color of candy form a group. In turn, ask each group member to introduce himself and then share one interesting fact about himself. Repeat until each child has met all his classmates.

Cathy Ogg
Happy Valley Elementary
Carter County, TN

Biopoem Project

Get the scoop on your new students with a winning first-day poetry project. Use the formula below to model the writing of a biopoem about yourself. Then have each child follow the formula to write a similar poem about herself. Finally, guide students through the steps provided to display their poems in a unique way.

Materials for each student:

wire clothes hanger, bent into an oval shape
large sheet of skin-toned tissue paper
glue
scissors
various art materials (colorful paper scraps, yarn, fabric, buttons, etc.)
pair of skin-toned paper hands and arms

Steps:

1. Cut the tissue paper in half.
2. Apply glue to the rim of the hanger. Place the glued rim facedown on one of the tissue paper halves.
3. Apply glue to the other side of the hanger. Press the remaining tissue paper half to the rim. Allow to dry overnight.
4. Trim the extra paper from the outside edge of the hanger.
5. Turn the hanger so that its hook is at the top. Decorate the oval with art materials to resemble your face.
6. Glue paper hands and arms to each side of the oval to hold your poem.

Kim Clasquin—Gr. 4
Garrett Elementary
Hazelwood, MO

Anna
Spunky, artistic, athletic, bright
Sister of Andy
Lover of theme parks, board games, and soccer
Who feels nervous on the first day of school, thrilled when I score a goal, and happy when I'm with my family
Who needs time to clean my room, money for my brother's birthday present, and to watch less TV
Who gives bread to ducks, hugs to my family, and cookies to my friends
Who fears snakes, lightning, and needles
Who would like to kick a game-winning soccer goal, see a movie on Saturday, and visit a friend on Sunday
Resident of St. Louis on Appletree Lane
Harrison

Biopoem

Line 1	First name only
Line 2	Four traits that describe yourself
Line 3	Brother/sister of…(or son/daughter of)
Line 4	Lover of…(three things)
Line 5	Who feels…(three things)
Line 6	Who needs…(three things)
Line 7	Who gives…(three things)
Line 8	Who fears…(three things)
Line 9	Who would like to…(three things)
Line 10	Resident of (your city) on (your street)
Line 11	Last name only

A Letter to Me

Start the new year—and end it—with this simple self-esteem booster. On the first day of school, have each student write a letter to himself expressing his goals for the year and listing ten positive things about himself. Collect the letters. On the last day of school, return each letter, to which you've added a note congratulating its owner for the goals he reached during the school year. A letter-perfect start, a letter-perfect ending!

Sr. Ann Claire Rhoads, St. Ann Catholic School, Fayetteville, NC

Getting-to-Know-You Graphs

Get to know your class with a first-day graphing activity that really stacks up! In advance, label each of several sheets of graph paper with a topic, such as "Number of Siblings," "Favorite Color," "Type of Pet," etc. Label each graph's axes appropriately. Post the graphs on a bulletin board titled "[Grade level taught] Graders Really Stack Up!" On the first day of school, provide each student with enough small stickers so that he can place one on each graph. When students are finished, have the class help you evaluate the data on the resulting bar graphs.

Kimberly Minafo—Gr. 4
Tooker Avenue Elementary
West Babylon, NY

Favorite Color

This Year I Want to...

...join 4-H club.
...read 25 new books.
...learn about tornadoes.
...make honor roll.
...learn about dinosaurs.

Jane

A Hands-Down Favorite

Learn what your students want to accomplish this year with a first-day activity that's sure to be a hands-down favorite! Have each child trace her hand on a sheet of paper. Direct her to write "This Year I Want to…" at the top of the paper. On each finger of the tracing, have her write something she wants to learn or accomplish during the school year. Then have her personalize the tracing with colorful drawings that illustrate some of her favorite things. Display students' completed papers on a bulletin board. Then send them home with the students' first batch of graded papers. What a "hand-y" way for you—and parents—to learn about your kids' goals!

Tammie M. Guidry—Gr. 5, Iota Elementary, Iota, LA

Missing-Piece Puzzles

Use this hands-on activity on the first day to show students how important it is to cooperate with others and ask for help. In advance, cut a variety of pictures from old magazines (one picture per student). Laminate the pictures; then cut each one into several puzzle pieces. Put all the pieces of a picture inside a plastic resealable bag; then take out one piece and place it in a bag that holds a different puzzle. Continue in this manner until each bag contains a puzzle with one missing piece and one piece that does not belong.

On the first day of school, give each student a bag of puzzle pieces to assemble. When a child discovers that a piece of his puzzle is missing and the extra piece doesn't work, suggest that he ask his classmates for help. Then watch as students happily complete their puzzles with a little help from their friends!

Barbara Samuels, Riverview School, Denville, NJ

Magnifying Glass Pattern

Use with "Guess Who!" on page 45.

Beaded Necklace Glyphs

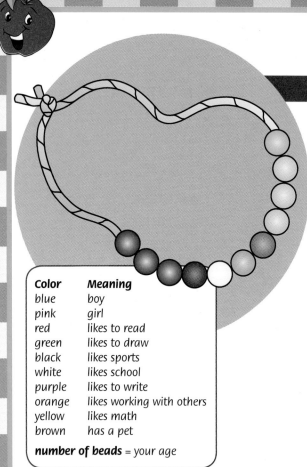

Color	Meaning
blue	boy
pink	girl
red	likes to read
green	likes to draw
black	likes sports
white	likes school
purple	likes to write
orange	likes working with others
yellow	likes math
brown	has a pet

number of beads = your age

Bead your way to a better-acquainted class with this cool activity! Obtain a supply of colorful craft beads (see the chart) and arrange them by color on a table. Display a chart like the one shown. Tell students that by stringing beads, they can communicate interesting facts about themselves, depending on the color and number of beads they use (for example, three beads of a color equals a greater interest in the subject than just one). After the discussion, give each student a 24-inch length of yarn. Call several children at a time to the table. Direct each child to string beads on his yarn to show his age and his interests. Then have him tie the necklace around his neck. As students admire their handiwork, you're sure to hear comments such as "Three yellow beads! You must really like math!" and "Look! We both like sports!"

Jeri Daugherity—Gr. 5
Mother Seton School
Emmitsburg, MD

First-Day Puzzles

Introduce yourself to your new class—and your students to one another—with an activity that's big on writing. In advance, write a brief paragraph about yourself on the bottom half of a sheet of paper. Underline 15 or more key words in the paragraph. Above the paragraph, create a word-search puzzle that includes the underlined words. Make a copy of the page for each student. On the first day of school, give each student a copy of the page to read and complete. Follow up by having each child create a similar page about himself. After each child shares his paragraph with the class, collect and laminate the papers. Then place them in a center along with a wipe-off marker so students can solve the puzzles during free time.

Joanie Brillant—Gr. 4
Bechtel Elementary
Okinawa, Japan

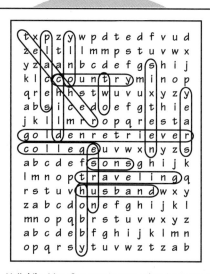

Hello! I'm Mrs. Cox, your new <u>teacher</u>. I grew up in the <u>country</u>. I was an <u>only child</u>. Growing up, I thought about becoming a <u>nurse</u>. But in <u>college</u>, I decided to become a teacher. I have taught for <u>sixteen years</u>. I have a <u>husband</u>, <u>two sons</u>, and a <u>golden retriever</u> named Taffy. My hobby is <u>traveling</u> to different <u>places</u> in the United States and the world.

From Interviews to License Plates

Give students the license to get to know one another better with this fun interviewing activity! First, pair each student with a classmate she does not know well. Have each partner interview the other, asking questions such as "What symbol would you choose to represent yourself and why?" and "What's your favorite number?" Next, give each child a 5½" x 9" sheet of white paper on which to design a license plate that tells about her partner (see the example). Provide time for students to share their plates. Then post the projects on a bulletin board decorated with cutout magazine pictures of cars and other vehicles.

J. Royce Brunk
Seoul Foreign School
Seoul, Korea

Tissue Introductions

For a get-acquainted game that your new students will really tear into, grab a roll of toilet tissue. As each student enters your room on the first day, tell him that the class will be playing a game later and to tear off as many sheets of tissue as he thinks he'll need in order to play. After the last child arrives, announce that the game requires each student to tell the class one thing about himself for each sheet of tissue he tore off the roll. Begin by modeling the activity yourself; then proceed around the room until each student has had a turn.

Julie Plowman—Gr. 6
Adair-Casey Elementary
Adair, IA

Personality Plates

Start the year—and end it—with this getting-to-know-you activity. Give each student a paper plate labeled with her name and an old newspaper or magazine. Direct the student to personalize her plate with cutout words that describe her. Allow each child to share her plate with the class; then post the plate on a bulletin board titled "Personality Plates." After you take down the display, store the plates until the end of the school year. On the last day of school, return each plate to its owner. Then have each student think about how she has changed over the year and share which words she would add or delete.

Steve Battles—Grs. 4–5
Butler Elementary
Springfield, IL

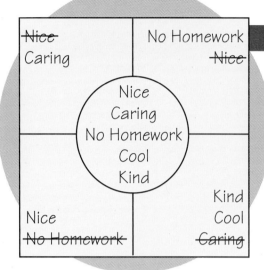

"Perfect Teacher" Want Ads

To minimize teacher and student anxiety on the first day of school, try reading *The Teacher From the Black Lagoon* by Mike Thaler. After reading, place the students in groups of four to brainstorm qualities they think characterize the perfect teacher. Have the groups use large, placemat-type graphic organizers like the one shown to record their ideas. Instruct each student to list his ideas on a corner of the placemat; then have the group combine the ideas in the circle. Next, have the groups write and illustrate want ads for the perfect teacher. Read several examples of want ads from the newspaper to get things started. Wrap up the activity by having the groups share their ads.

Candace J. Adams
Houston, TX

Getting to Know *Us!*

Getting to know each other was never easier than with this data-collecting and graph-building activity! Provide each student with a large, lined index card. Assign each child one topic from the list shown to write at the top of her card. On the first line of the card, have the student write the information about herself that matches the topic, plus her name. Then direct her to lay the card on her desk.

Next, allow students several minutes to circulate around the room writing their responses and names on each card. Collect the cards and divide students into groups of three. Then give each group three of the cards and a 12" x 18" sheet of white paper. Direct each group to create and illustrate a graph that depicts the information listed on each of its cards. When the graphs are completed, display them on a bulletin board titled "Here's Looking at Us!"

Two Hobbies I Enjoy	
read, soccer	Samantha
reading, skating	Kimberly
drawing, photography	Lamont
basketball, soccer	Matt
gymnastics, baseball	Sallie

Card Topics

- my favorite video game
- the number of pets I have
- my favorite summer vacation spot
- my favorite kind of book
- my favorite dessert
- my favorite musical group
- my favorite TV show
- my favorite holiday
- my three favorite pizza toppings
- the kinds of pets I have
- my favorite flavor of ice cream
- the color of my eyes
- the number of letters in my full name
- my favorite kind of car
- two hobbies I enjoy
- the state I was born in
- the number of brothers and sisters I have
- my usual weekday bedtime
- my favorite restaurant
- two of my favorite sports
- my favorite season of the year

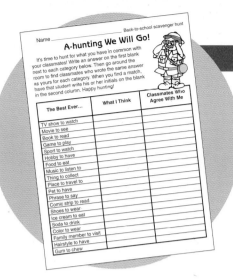

A-hunting We Will Go!

Foster an environment in which feelings of familiarity and acceptance can grow with this back-to-school scavenger hunt. Give each student a copy of the bottom half of page 58 to complete as directed. Afterward, bring the class together to analyze the results, asking questions such as the following:

- Which categories were the easiest to match?
- Did you find a match for every category? If you didn't, is that important? Why?
- What things did you have in common with your classmates?
- Which findings surprised you?

You can bet that everyone will know his classmates better after this extraordinary excursion!

Daniel Kriesberg—Gr. 4
Locust Valley Intermediate School
Locust Valley, NY

Bits and Pieces About Me

Help students get to know one another with a unique, high-flying display! If available, hang a few colorful kites in the upper corners of your classroom. Give each student a large kite pattern divided into 12 numbered segments as shown. Post the following directions on a large chart; then set students free to color their unique kites. Explain that if both colors in a direction apply to them, students should color that block with a design that uses both colors. Have students decorate the backs of their kites with stylized versions of their names or initials. Encourage students to add kite tails, including one paper or fabric bow for each family member (including pets). Suspend the kites from the classroom ceiling with fishing line. Students will soar into the new year while learning all about their classmates!

Directions:
1. Color section one red if you're a girl and blue if you're a boy.
2. Color section two yellow if you're an only child and green if you have brothers and/or sisters.
3. Color section three blue if you have a pet and green if you don't.
4. Color section four purple if this is your first year at this school and pink if you've been at this school for more than a year.
5. Color section five orange if you play on a sports team and red if you are involved in a non-sports afterschool activity.
6. Color section six green if you've always lived in this state and red if you've ever lived in another state.
7. Color section seven blue if you have your own bedroom and yellow if you share a bedroom with someone.
8. Color section eight green if you like math and orange if you like writing.
9. Color section nine purple if you prefer working with a group and red if you prefer working alone.
10. Color section ten blue if you like winter and yellow if you like summer.
11. Color section eleven green if you prefer being a listener and red if you prefer being a speaker.
12. Color section twelve orange if you like television and green if you like books.

Sara L. Ertl—Gr. 5
Lehigh Elementary
Palmerton, PA

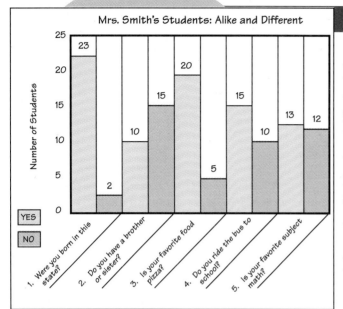

Mrs. Smith's Students: Alike and Different

Number of Students

	YES	NO
1. Were you born in this state?	23	2
2. Do you have a brother or sister?	10	15
3. Is your favorite food pizza?	20	5
4. Do you ride the bus to school?	15	10
5. Is your favorite subject math?	13	12

Getting-to-Know-You Poll

Use this icebreaking activity to help your students appreciate how they are alike and different. Begin by writing five yes-or-no questions on the board, such as the ones shown on the graph. (Avoid questions that would group students by gender or along racial or cultural lines.) Ask each student to number his paper from 1 to 5; then have him answer the questions. After collecting the papers, display the results of the poll in a simple double-bar graph as shown. Next, have students help you label a large sheet of chart paper with several statements based on the poll. (For example, you might write "Most of us were born in this state. Five students don't consider pizza their favorite food.") Then have each student write a paragraph describing the benefits of having classmates who are both alike and different.

Lisa Waller Rogers
Austin, TX

Heads Above the Rest

Want each of your kids to feel like she's heads above the rest? Using an overhead projector, project the silhouette of each student's head onto construction paper and trace it. Have each child cut out magazine pictures of objects or activities she enjoys; then have her glue them collage-style within her outline. Next, have the student cut out her silhouette and glue it onto a piece of poster board. Circulate the finished posters, asking each child to write a compliment on every classmate's poster. Encourage students to be specific in their compliments, such as "I like your smile" or "You're a great soccer player." Laminate the signed posters; then display one each week before sending it home with the proud owner.

Teresa Munson—Grs. 4–5, R–9 North Elementary, Warsaw, MO

Zingo!

In need of a new icebreaker for that first day of school? Provide the class with bingo markers, such as dried beans or popcorn kernels. Then have each child complete a copy of the game card on page 59 by filling in the blanks. Call on one student at a time to read aloud a sentence from his card. Cross out that sentence on your own copy of the page. Then direct students whose answers match the one read to cover that space with a marker. When a student covers five spaces in a row, have him call out, "Zingo!" Then check his answers by having him read aloud those five sentences. If correct, declare him the winner. Zingo!

Julia Alarie—Gr. 6, Essex Middle School, Essex, VT

New-Class Gallery

Get to know your students better with an art and writing project that becomes a decorative display! First, use a favorite computer program to print a graphic of an attractive picture frame. Make a copy of the picture frame for each student, leaving space below the frame for the student to write a paragraph. Direct each student to draw and color a picture of herself doing something she enjoys in the space inside the frame. Then have her add a paragraph about her likes, dislikes, hobbies, and family in the space below the frame. Direct the student to share her work with the class. Then arrange the papers along a classroom wall to create a picture-perfect gallery of your new class!

Neal Dickstein—Gr. 5
Ethel McKnight School
East Windsor, NJ

Into the Swim of Things

Dive into a new school year with this fishy art project! Give each student a sheet of 8½" x 11" white paper. Have the student draw a large fish shape; then have her write her name in bubble or block letters inside the outline before cutting out the fish. Post a color key as shown. Have the student use markers and crayons to personalize her fish according to her choices from the key. Display each student's fish and the key on a bulletin board that you've covered with blue paper and titled "We're Back Into the Swim of Things!"

Joan M. Macey
Binghamton, NY

All-About-Me Key

Subjects I like (body):
math = yellow
social studies = purple
science = green
reading = red

Hobbies (tail):
computer = pink
sports = brown
music = blue
art = orange

Family (scales; one per item):
sister = pink triangle
brother = blue triangle
cat = orange circle
dog = black circle
other pet = green triangle

Food Favorites (fins):
pizza = red
fries = yellow
tacos = green
burgers = brown

I enjoy playing football.

Josh
Dylan
Megan
Lauren
Garrett

My favorite subject is reading.

Ashley
Emily
Katherine
Hollis
Joseph

Common Bonds

Searching for a first-day-of-school activity that's uncommonly fun? Label each of several sheets of paper with a different simple sentence that states a topic of interest, such as "My favorite subject is reading" or "I enjoy playing football." Place a different sheet on each student's desk. Direct students to move about the room and read the sentence at the top of each sheet. Then have each child sign every sheet with which he agrees. After all signing is completed, share the lists with students. They'll be amazed to see all the common bonds they share with their new classmates!

Nellie Mullins—Gr. 4
Belle Reynolds Elementary
Oakfield, WI

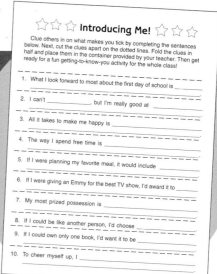

☆☆☆ **Introducing Me!** ☆☆☆

Clue others in on what makes you tick by completing the sentences below. Next, cut the clues apart on the dotted lines. Fold the clues in half and place them in the container provided by your teacher. Then get ready for a fun getting-to-know-you activity for the whole class!

1. What I look forward to most about the first day of school is _____
2. I can't _____, but I'm really good at _____
3. All it takes to make me happy is _____
4. The way I spend free time is _____
5. If I were planning my favorite meal, it would include _____
6. If I were giving an Emmy for the best TV show, I'd award it to _____
7. My most prized possession is _____
8. If I could be like another person, I'd choose _____
9. If I could own only one book, I'd want it to be _____
10. To cheer myself up, I _____

Stand Up and Be Recognized!

Spark new friendships and build camaraderie with this easy getting-to-know-you activity. Have each student complete the reproducible on the top half of page 58; then have her cut out the clues, fold them in half, and place them in a container provided by you. Each day during the first week of school, gather students in a large circle on the floor and read aloud ten to 20 clues, one at a time. After you read each clue, direct its writer to stand. As clues are read, your students will quickly identify classmates with whom they share something in common. What an uncommonly great icebreaker!

Joy A. Kalfas
Palatine, IL

A Map of Me

Find out what makes your students tick—and how much geography they remember from last year—with this mapmaking activity. First, have the class study a variety of maps to review their common attributes: a compass rose, bodies of water, natural or political boundaries, etc. Next, ask a student to share with the class his hobbies, favorite foods and activities, and other interesting facts about himself. As he speaks, organize his responses on the board as shown above, assigning each interest a geographic name.

Next, challenge each student to organize his own interests in a similar organizer. When the organizer is finished, have him cut a 24" x 36" sheet of construction paper into a simple shape that reflects one of his interests, such as a basketball, computer screen, or skate. Then have the student use art materials and his organizer to transform the cutout into a map of himself. Post the maps on a bulletin board titled "A Map of Me!"

Merrill Watrous
Eugene, OR

The Land of Juan Garcia

Bodies of Water — Lake Michael Jordan, Soccer Kid Highway, Chocolate River
Roads — Baseball Fan Road
Landforms — Maria Mountains, Skating Hills
Cities — Computerburg, Ice Creamville

No Need to Be Puzzled About Me!

Directions:
1. Fill in the blanks using your best handwriting.
2. Lightly color each puzzle piece with a crayon or colored pencil. Color lightly enough so that your answers can still be read.
3. Cut out the puzzle pieces; then place them in an envelope labeled with your name.
4. Trade envelopes with a classmate.
5. Put your classmate's puzzle together and read all about him or her; then put the pieces back in the envelope and trade with another classmate.

Name: _____

Age: _____ Birthdate: _____

I have _____ people in my family. Their names are: _____ .

The best thing I did this summer was _____

_____

One thing I wish I had done this summer was _____

My favorite color is _____ . My favorite food is _____

In my free time I like to _____

My favorite school subject is _____ . My least favorite subject is _____

I get upset when _____

When I get older I'd like to work as a _____

If I could do anything, I'd like to _____

_____

If I could live anywhere in the world, I would live in _____ because

_____

The most interesting thing I've ever done is _____

_____

The person I most admire is _____ because _____

_____

The best thing about me is _____

_____

I am a good friend because _____

The first day of school is very _____ because _____

_____

©The Mailbox® • *Back-to-School* • TEC1499

Note to the teacher: Duplicate this page onto white construction paper for each student. Provide each student with an envelope, scissors, and crayons or colored pencils.

Back-to-school scavenger hunt

A-hunting We Will Go!

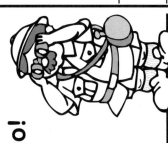

It's time to hunt for what you have in common with your classmates! Write an answer on the first blank next to each category below. Then go around the room to find classmates who wrote the same answer as yours for each category. When you find a match, have that student write his or her initials on the blank in the second column. Happy hunting!

The Best Ever...	What I Think	Classmates Who Agree With Me
TV show to watch		
Movie to see		
Book to read		
Game to play		
Sport to watch		
Hobby to have		
Food to eat		
Music to listen to		
Thing to collect		
Place to travel to		
Pet to have		
Phrase to say		
Comic strip to read		
Shoes to wear		
Ice cream to eat		
Soda to drink		
Color to wear		
Family member to visit		
Hairstyle to have		
Gum to chew		

©The Mailbox® • *Back-to-School* • TEC1499

Note to the teacher: Use with "A-hunting We Will Go!" on page 53.

☆ ☆ ☆ ☆ ☆ ☆ ☆ **Introducing Me!**

Clue others in on what makes you tick by completing the sentences below. Next, cut the clues apart on the dotted lines. Fold the clues in half and place them in the container provided by your teacher. Then get ready for a fun getting-to-know-you activity for the whole class!

1. What I look forward to most about the first day of school is _____.

2. I can't _____, but I'm really good at _____.

3. All it takes to make me happy is _____.

4. The way I spend free time is _____.

5. If I were planning my favorite meal, it would include _____.

6. If I were giving an Emmy for the best TV show, I'd award it to _____.

7. My most prized possession is _____.

8. If I could be like another person, I'd choose _____.

9. If I could own only one book, I'd want it to be _____.

10. To cheer myself up, I _____.

©The Mailbox® • *Back-to-School* • TEC1499

Note to the teacher: Use with "Stand Up and Be Recognized!" on page 56.

Z I N G O

Z	I	N	G	O
For fun, I like to ___ .	My eye color is ___ .	The street I live on is ___ .	I (can/cannot) speak another language. ¡HOLA!	I have a pet ___ .
My favorite song is ___ .	I usually ___ (bring/buy) my lunch.	My lucky number is ___ .	My favorite grade so far is ___ .	I have ___ brothers and sisters.
My favorite color is ___ .	My career goal is to become a(n) ___ .	My favorite relative is my ___ .	If I had my own car, it would be a(n) ___ 4-ME	I wish my first name was ___ .
I was born in ___ (city). It's A Girl! It's A Boy!	My favorite subject in school is ___ .	I'd like to buy a(n) ___ .	My birthday is in the month of ___ .	I ___ (have/have not) visited another country.
My favorite time of day is ___ o'clock.	My favorite movie is ___ .	My favorite season of the year is ___ .	My favorite food is ___ .	The best book I have ever read is ___ .

Note to the teacher: Use with "Zingo!" on page 54.

59

Jan.	Feb.	Mar.	Apr.
6 Liani			4 Kate
9 Scott	2 Gary		12 Efren
23 Meg	5 Jill		24 Mark
27 Clint	11 Nia	6 Kyle	30 Lucy

Birthday Cupcakes

Keeping up with birthdays for 25 or more students can be overwhelming. To make this an easier task, create a chart with a column for each month of the year on a bulletin board. Before the first day of school, make a blank cupcake for each student. Have the student write his name and the day of his birthday on his cupcake; then have him color his cupcake. Next, have the students staple their cupcakes in the correct columns on the board. This is a great introductory activity to a graphing unit as well as a quick reference for each child's birthday.

Sarah Young—Gr. 5
Haw Creek School
Asheville, NC

Birthday Boost

This project works wonders with boosting self-esteem and peer cooperation. At the beginning of the school year, set up celebration clubs. These are groups of three or four students who are in charge of decorating a classmate's locker or desk with balloons, streamers, banners, and cards on her birthday. The celebration club changes once a month so that everyone gets to participate. With this birthday booster, students learn that giving can be as much fun as receiving.

Jodi Tuskowski—Grs. 5–6
Madison Elementary
Stevens Point, WI

The Birthday Bag

Wishing you could celebrate birthdays in your classroom without breaking the bank? Just fill a birthday gift bag with free items from book club orders and children's fast-food meals or inexpensive gifts from a local dollar store. On a student's special day, let him select an item from your birthday bag.

Teresa Vilfer-Snyder—Gr. 4
Fredericktown Intermediate School
Fredericktown, OH

Birthday Bulletin Board

Recycle used foil balloons to decorate a birthday bulletin board. Attach colorful ribbon to each balloon and arrange the bunch as shown. On the first day of school, have each student write his name and birthdate on a paper cutout balloon. Add the approriate student balloons to the foil display at the beginning of each month.

Marion Young—Gr. 4
Weigelstown Elementary
Dover, PA

Mark the Day!

Don't forget a single student's birthday with this handy tip. A few days before the start of a new month, ask each student celebrating a birthday that month to place a sticker in the appropriate box on your class calendar. Allow each summer birthday student to place her sticker on any day of a month of her choice. One quick glance at your calendar and you'll be ready to croon "Happy Birthday"!

Julie Granchelli
Lockport, NY

Class Birthday Basket

Make a student's birthday extra special with this gift idea. Program slips of paper with one-day class privileges, such as "Sit at any desk you wish" or "Choose your place in line." Gift-wrap each slip inside a jewelry-size box. Then place the gifts in a basket. On a child's birthday, allow her to choose a gift from the basket. If her birthday falls on a weekend or during a school break, let her pick her gift the day before. For students with summer birthdays, have them choose their gifts during the last week of school.

Cathy Ogg
Elizabethton, TN

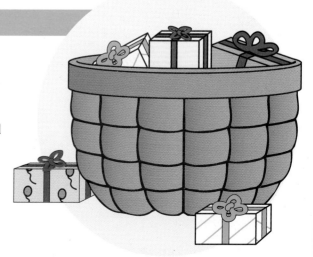

Good-Luck Penny

This special birthday wish is worth its weight in gold! Whenever a student has a birthday, tape a penny, dated with the year of the student's birth, onto a sticky note. Then write a birthday wish on the note and stick it to the student's desk. Students will cherish their good-luck pennies!

Jackie Strack—Gr. 4
Geary Elementary
Geary, OK

Birthday Bonanza

At the beginning of the year, provide each student with a birthday cake pattern. Have each child color and cut out her cake; then have her write her name, birthday, and favorite candy bar on the back. Collect the cakes and arrange them in chronological order. Also list all of the birthdays on your yearly planning calendar. When a birthday draws near, write that student's name and birthday on the decorated side of her cake; then post the cake on your birthday bulletin board. On the student's special day, present her with a gift of the candy bar listed on the back of her cake!

Suzanne Whitehurst—Gr. 5
Lake Magdalene Elementary
Tampa, FL

Birthday Placards

At the start of the school year, give each child a 4" x 9" sheet of construction paper. Have the student write her name and birthdate on the paper. Then have her use paint, glitter, or other media to decorate the remaining space with birthday illustrations. Collect and store these placards. Then, each month, bring the appropriate placard(s) out of storage to display on a bulletin board. Students will enjoy looking at each other's birthday placards and remembering how they decorated their own.

Eleanor Messner
Lachawanna Trail Elementary Center
Dalton, PA

Once-a-Month Celebrations

If group birthday celebrations are more to your school's liking than individual ones, then this idea is for you! At the beginning of each month, create a schoolwide display showing photos of students who will celebrate birthdays during that month. If desired, include information contributed by the birthday kids themselves. Next, schedule a day on which parent volunteers can bring snacks for the birthday kids to enjoy at a special group gathering. If desired, distribute small treats such as pencils, erasers, or other school supplies. During the celebration, introduce each birthday child; then sing "Happy Birthday" together. Include children with July birthdays in the August (or September) celebration and those with June birthdays in the May festivities.

Gratsiela Sabangan—Grs. 4–6
Three Angels School
Wichita, KS

Birthday Goodie Bags

Make students feel special on their birthdays with this unbeatable gift idea! During the summer, fill colorful birthday bags with inexpensive dime-store goodies. When school rolls around, place the bags in a large container labeled "Happy Birthday!" On each student's birthday, surprise him with a goodie bag. You'll start a tradition that's guaranteed to make every birthday a happy one!

Heidi Graves—Gr. 4
Wateree Elementary
Lugoff, SC

Cool Fridge Facts!

What's the prime location in a student's home to post school news? On the fridge, of course! Every Friday afternoon, give each student a copy of page 67. Have the child list next week's vocabulary words, as well as information about upcoming tests, projects, activities, and other important events. In the notes section, instruct her to write about a goal she is working toward, a skill she is developing, or a project that's in the works. Ask each child to return her fridge facts sheet on the following Friday signed by a parent. What a cool way to keep parents in the know!

Kimberly Minafo—Gr. 4
Tooker Avenue Elementary
West Babylon, NY

COOL FRIDGE FACTS

for the week of _____
Student's name: _____

This week's vocabulary words:

I can...
spell it   define it   use it in two good sentences

1. _____
2. _____
3. _____
4. _____
5. _____
6. _____
7. _____
8. _____
9. _____
10. _____

This week:

- We'll be working on _____ in language arts.
- In math, we will _____
- Our current science unit is about _____
- In social studies, we will learn about _____
- As a class, we are reading the book _____
- Independently, I am reading _____

Important dates and notes:
_____
_____
_____
_____

Signed by: _____

Monday Newsletter

Put a twist on the standard Friday newsletter with this simple (and smart!) idea. Provide your students and parents with a weekly newsletter each Monday instead of at the end of the week. Include sections labeled "School Happenings for the Week," "This Week's Classroom Events," "Student Birthdays," "Curriculum Activities," "Special Recognitions," and "Help Needed." With this tip, both parents and students will be fully prepared for the great week ahead!

Lori Brandman—Gr. 5
Shallowford Falls Elementary
Marietta, GA

Connie Fields   555-0178
Maggie Fields
Douglas Fields   Same

Logging Parent Contacts

Keep track of parent contacts with hassle-free ease using this simple system. First, make a label for each student that includes her name, parents' names, and home phone number(s). Affix each label to the outside of a pocket folder. Inside the folder, keep a log of all parent contacts, as well as copies of any notes that you send home. This system eliminates lost phone number lists and makes it easy for you to document parent contacts.

Angela Wood-Hurst
Lewis and Clark Middle School
Tulsa, OK

#58—November 20
If your food could talk, what would you say to it? Create a conversation you could have with your meal at dinnertime.

Journal-Prompt Newsletters

Create a class newsletter that's anything but ordinary with the help of your daily journal prompts. Assign a number to each day's prompt as shown. Have each student include that number along with the date and his name when he responds to the prompt in his journal. Then, as you prepare each newsletter, have each child submit to you the number and date of a journal entry from that week or any other time during the year. Pull the appropriate journal and add that child's entry into your class newsletter. The result is a newsletter that both parents and students will find hard to put down!

Melissa Wood—Gr. 4
Memorial Day School
Savannah, GA

Math Newsletters

Make math concepts taught at school crystal clear to parents by creating hot-off-the-press math newsletters just for them! Each time you begin to teach a new math concept, send home a newsletter that explains each objective and the recommended teaching procedure. Also include sample problems, games, and hands-on activities that parents can use to reinforce the concept at home. Parents will appreciate your efforts, and students will get the same instruction from parents that they get at school!

Julie Granchelli
Lockport, NY

Fabulous Photo Newsletters

If a picture is worth a thousand words, then why not include one or two in your class newsletter? At the beginning of the year, create a newsletter template that has sections such as the following:
- newsletter's title, the date, and a place for a photo or clip art
- "In Class This Week" (an overview of units being studied and dates of scheduled tests)
- "FYI" (miscellaneous information and dates of field trips or other special events)

Each time your class does something especially interesting, capture that moment with your school's digital camera. Save all of the photos on a disk. Each Friday, download a current photo into the template and update the weekly information; then print the newsletter and make photocopies. In just a matter of minutes, your fab photo newsletter is ready for students to take home. Be sure to hand a copy to your principal to keep her updated about what's going on in your classroom too.

Debra Wilham—Gr. 4
Mt. Pulaski Elementary
Mt. Pulaski, IL

It's in the Mail!

Make keeping in touch with parents a little easier this year! Have parents, grandparents, and/or other caregivers send large, pre-addressed, stamped envelopes to school. Let each student put her favorite papers or artwork in her envelope; then mail the envelopes. It's an easy way to make sure a great paper actually makes it home in one piece!

Melinda Salisbury—Grs. 4–6
Baldwin North Intermediate
Quincy, IL

Postcards From Home

Want to start building a strong home-school connection right from the start? On back-to-school night, send each family home with a supply of stamped postcards addressed to you at school. Invite parents to send you postcards throughout the year sharing their child's special accomplishments. Post the cards on a special bulletin board in your classroom. Students will love reading these kudos from home!

Kimberly A. Minafo—Gr. 4
Tooker Avenue School
West Babylon, NY

Newsletter Reading Incentive

How can you know whether the newsletters you send home are being read? Find out with this nifty idea! At the bottom of each newsletter, include a special coupon, such as the one shown, that can be cut out and redeemed at school if it has been filled out and signed by a parent. Be sure to make each reward so appealing that students who do not participate one week will want to do so the next!

Julie Granchelli
Lockport, NY

COOL FRIDGE FACTS

for the week of _____

Student's name: _____

This week's vocabulary words:

I can...

	spell it	define it	use it in two good sentences
1. _____	_____	_____	_____
2. _____	_____	_____	_____
3. _____	_____	_____	_____
4. _____	_____	_____	_____
5. _____	_____	_____	_____
6. _____	_____	_____	_____
7. _____	_____	_____	_____
8. _____	_____	_____	_____
9. _____	_____	_____	_____
10. _____	_____	_____	_____

This week:

- We'll be working on _____ in **language arts.**
- In **math,** we will _____.
- Our current **science** unit is about _____.
- In **social studies,** we will learn about _____.
- As a class, **we are reading** the book _____.
- Independently, **I am reading** _____.

Important dates and notes:

_____

_____

_____

_____

_____

Signed by: _____

Note to the teacher: Use with "Cool Fridge Facts!" on page 64.

Guest Book

As parents arrive for open house, ask them to write their names and addresses in a classroom guest book. Take lots of pictures throughout the evening. When you have the film developed, request double prints. Add one set of prints to the guest book, and send the others home in thank-you cards written by the students. With this idea, everyone has a memento of open house!

Linda Stroik—Gr. 4
Jackson Elementary
Stevens Point, WI

May We Quote You?

Involve the whole family in this writing project—and create a bulletin board that's perfect for open house! About a week or two before your scheduled open house, send home a reproducible asking parents and other family members to complete the sentence "I've learned that..." Include a sample or two, such as "I've learned that most of the things I worry about never happen." Ask each family to send as many quotes as it would like. Post all responses on a "May We Quote You?" bulletin board for visitors to enjoy during open house.

Brenda H. McGee—Gr. 4
Meadows Elementary
Plano, TX

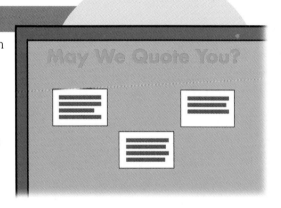

And the Winner Is...

Motivate an interest in open house by awarding some simple door prizes. Decorate your classroom with inexpensive houseplants or flower arrangements. At the close of open house, have each guest drop his nametag in a box. Then draw names and award the plants to the winning parents. Reward the child of each lucky parent with a book, homemade gift, or other small item.

Patricia Dancho—Gr. 6 Language Arts
Apollo-Ridge Middle School
Spring Church, PA

Debbie Schneck—Gr. 4
Fogelsville Elementary
Schnecksville, PA

"Guess Who!" Wall

This display will be a real eye-catcher for the students, parents, and staff at your school. Ask each student to bring to class a baby picture and a recent photo of herself. Attach each student's baby photo to the outside of a folded sheet of pink or blue construction paper. Then attach the recent photo to the inside. Have students add their signatures and colorful decorations around their recent photos. Display these folded sheets on the wall outside your classroom. Everyone who visits at open house will love to guess who's who!

Susan Giesie—Gr. 4
Ben Franklin School
Menomonee Falls, WI

We love to...

Graffiti Charts

For open house, hang several pieces of colorful bulletin board paper outside your classroom. On each one write a sentence starter such as "We love to…," "The funniest thing that ever happened was…," and "I really like it when my parent/child…" Place a bucket of colorful markers nearby; then invite parents and their children to fill the charts with their responses.

Debbie Schneck—Gr. 4
Fogelsville Elementary
Schnecksville, PA

Snappy Silhouettes

To create an eye-catching open house display, use an overhead projector to make a silhouette of each student in your class. With a white pencil, outline each child's profile on black paper; then cut out the silhouette, mount it onto white paper, and frame it with red paper strips. Attach these silhouettes to students' chairs to "greet" parents at open house.

Nancy Barra—Gr. 5
McCormick Elementary
Chicago, IL

Boxed In

For a fun back-to-school art project, ask each student to bring an empty cardboard food box to class. Have students cover their boxes with colorful construction paper. On each of the four sides of the box, a student writes and illustrates a positive statement about himself. Then he attaches a current snapshot of himself to the top of the box. These completed boxes make a great display for open house!

Nancy Thorrington—Grs. 5–6
Burt Township School
Grand Marais, MI

Can You Find Me?

Encourage self-expression with this colorful back-to-school art activity. On an 8½" x 11" sheet of white construction paper, have each student create a personal collage with pictures cut from old magazines. Direct her to hide her picture or name somewhere in the collage and list five clues about the collage on an index card with her name. Collect the collages and cards; then arrange the collages in a giant square on a wall or bulletin board. Add students' names around the square and title the display "Can You Find Me?" At open house, give each parent her child's clue card. Challenge each parent to find her child's collage based on the clues.

Kim Marie Lennon—Gr. 4
Chestnut Hill Elementary
Dix Hills, NY

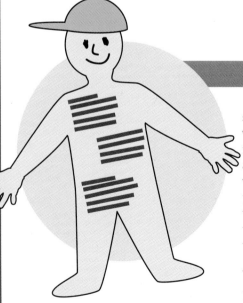

Open House Self-Portraits

During the first week of school, have students draw and cut out large, simple paper-doll patterns. On the body of the cutout, have each student write three paragraphs: a description of himself that includes hobbies, interests, and special talents; a paragraph describing what he hopes to accomplish during the school year; and a paragraph explaining how he views the world. Instruct each student to personalize and decorate his pattern so that it resembles himself. On the night of open house, display these paper-doll people in the classroom; then challenge parents to identify their children. Give the projects to parents to take home as keepsakes of their children's school year.

Theresa Hickey—Gr. 4
St. Ignatius School
Mobile, AL

Welcome, Mom and Dad!

A few days before open house, have students write letters to their parents. Place a copy of each student's letter in his portfolio. Then, on open house night, place each child's original letter on his desk. Parents will love these letters, which they can take home as keepsakes. At the end of the year, have each student write another letter—this time to a student in the next lower grade. Compare this letter to the one written earlier for open house. Students will be surprised and delighted to see how their writing has improved over the year.

Maxine Pincott—Gr. 4
Oliver Ellsworth School
Windsor, CT

Dear Mom and Dad,

Susie

It's in the Bag!

On the first day of school, have students create time capsules out of brown paper bags. Direct each student to fold down the top of her bag and decorate it with paper eyes, arms, and legs. Inside the capsule, have her place the following: a math facts quiz; a handwriting sample; an essay titled "What I Would Like to Learn by the End of the Year"; a list of known states, capitals, and continents; and a student photo. For open house, display the capsules on a bulletin board with the title "This Year Is in the Bag!" Afterward, store the bags until the end of the year. When students finally open them, they will be astounded at all that they've learned over the year!

Taryl M. Hargens—Gr. 4
Sacred Hearts School
Lahaina, Maui, HI

Quote Me on That!

This back-to-school activity sets up the perfect open house icebreaker. On the first day of school, have each student fill out an interest inventory. Select one quote from each student's paper and write it on a separate sentence strip. On open house night, place the strips on a table. As parents arrive, challenge them to find their child's quote. Open house will be a hit, and you'll have information about your students to personalize lessons throughout the school year!

Lisa Stephens—Gr. 5
Centerville Elementary
Anderson, SC

I know that has to be Jeremy's quote.

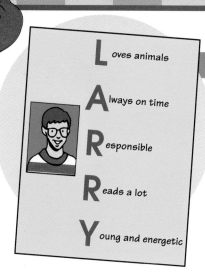

Begin With Acrostics

At the beginning of the school year, take snapshots of students in groups of two or three. Cut the photos so that each student has a picture of himself. Give each student a 6" x 9" sheet of construction paper on which to paste his picture. Instruct the child to write the letters of his name in a column beside the picture; then have him use each letter to begin a word or phrase that tells something about himself. Post the finished acrostics on a bulletin board titled "The World's Greatest Class!" Students will enjoy getting to know each other by reading their classmates' acrostics. Plus the board will make a great open house display!

Joyceann Dreibelbis—Gr. 4
Kean Elementary
Wooster, OH

Keeping Open House Open

Everyone can have a wonderful time at an open house that is casual and involves parents, students, and staff. Consider the following tips:

- If your chorus gives a presentation, include some sing-along numbers so everyone can join in.
- If you have a school band or orchestra, invite parents and teachers to bring their instruments and join in a concert.
- Have a dance for students, teachers, and parents.
- Set up carnival booths for older children to demonstrate math and science "magic."
- Invite everyone to activities in common areas such as the gym, cafeteria, or hallways.
- Try not to turn open house into a mini-conference time.
- Serve refreshments and make sure that open house is a real social event!

Julia Alarie—Gr. 6
Essex Middle School
Essex, VT

Collecting Classroom Supplies

At open house, mention to parents that your classroom is always in need of cups, plates, napkins, plastic utensils, etc. Then ask them to donate their extra party supplies. Remind parents that students don't mind eating off Fourth of July plates—even in August!

Lisa Borgo—Gr. 4
Gould Avenue School
North Caldwell, NJ

Hospitality Hosts

Let your students take charge of open house! Have each child place her books, folders, and portfolio on her desk at the end of the school day. Provide each student with a copy of a hospitality checklist (see the illustration) to use as an outline when her family arrives. On the night of open house, have students greet parents, describe important aspects of the classroom, and answer questions. You can sit in the background with parents and help when the need arises.

Phyllis Ellett—Grs. 3–4
Earl Hanson Elementary
Rock Island, IL

Open House
Make sure you see...
___ Daily journal
___ Reading folder
___ Portfolio
___ Art projects
___ Computer room
___ Science exhibit

Parent Packet for the Parents of James

Parent Packets

Give each parent who attends open house a colorful folder titled "Parent Packet for the Parents of [student's name]." Place inside each packet copies of newspaper and magazine articles relevant to education and parenting skills. Also include classroom rules, your homework policy, suggestions for encouraging reading at home, tips for assisting with schoolwork, and directions for sending work in case of absences. Also include brochures from local parks and community colleges in which you've highlighted events of interest to parents and their children. Parents will love getting these informative packets!

Patricia Novak—Gr. 4
Meadowbrook School
Eatontown, NJ

Getting-to-Know-Us Class Book

Start the year off "write" with this whole-class project! Give each student a sheet of unlined paper. Draw the format shown on the board and have each student copy it on his paper. (Direct students to leave a margin on the left side of the page for hole-punching later.) Instruct each student to bring a picture of himself to glue in the circle. Each morning, write one of the topics shown on the board. Then have each child write about the topic inside one of his page's sections. When all eight sections have been filled, have each student share his page with the class. Then collect the pages and punch three holes on the left side of each one. Bind the pages together with yarn, along with a cover signed by each student. Display the book during open house for parents to enjoy.

Julia Alarie—Gr. 6
Essex Middle School
Essex, VT

Topics:
• the most interesting experience of your life
• your plans for the future
• your family
• your hobbies, talents, pets, sports, and other interests
• your favorite books, foods, movies, TV shows, etc.
• your favorite school subjects and activities
• your best memory from past years of school
• your birthday, your birthplace, and places you've lived and visited

Letter Perfect!

Welcome parents and other visitors with these bright, colorful projects.

Materials for each student:

9" x 12" white construction paper
markers and crayons
glue
assorted decorations such as glitter,
  sequins, and yarn

pencil
scissors
black fine-tip marker

Steps:

1. Sketch the first letter of your first name on a 9" x 12" sheet of white construction paper. Make big block letters that fill the sheet.
2. Write the remainder of your name somewhere on the letter, making sure that it is readable; then outline the letter with a black fine-tip marker.
3. Cut out the letter.
4. Personalize the letter with symbols that represent your hobbies and interests. Use glitter, markers, crayons, sequins, yarn, and other available items for decoration.

Display all of the completed letters on a bulletin board or your classroom door.

Stained-Glass Names

Decorate your windows with this eye-catching stained-glass project.

Materials for each student:

clear plastic wrap (about 12" x 12")
piece of tagboard or other stiff paper (about 10" x 10")
paper clips
permanent markers (including assorted bright colors and black)

Steps:

1. Secure the plastic wrap to the tagboard with paper clips.
2. Use permanent markers to write your name (in fat, bubbly letters) on the plastic, using a different color for each letter.
3. Outline your name with a black permanent marker.
4. To complete the project, carefully cut around the black outline and then remove the paper clips and lift your name from the tagboard.
5. Adhere the stained-glass name to your classroom window. You may need to add a few drops of water to make the plastic wrap adhere to the glass.

Elizabeth Bourassa—Gr. 6
Olson School
Minneapolis, MN

Cool Suncatchers

Beautiful student-made suncatchers will brighten any classroom! Provide each student with an 8" x 8" paper square and an 8" x 8" piece of clear lightweight vinyl. First, have each student draw a simple design on the paper square. Next, have him lay his vinyl square over the design and outline the picture with a black fine-tip permanent marker. Finally, have the student turn over the vinyl and color in the design with permanent markers. Attach these suncatchers to your windows for months of viewing pleasure!

Heather Eubank—Gr. 5
Willow Brook Elementary
Creve Coeur, MO

Woven Initials

Help students learn more about one another—and practice the Native American art of weaving—with this attractive back-to-school art project!

Materials for each student:
one 9" x 12" sheet of black construction paper
   cut lengthwise into ½" strips
thirty ½" x 9" strips of construction paper
   (six of each of five different colors)
two 9" x 12" sheets of colored construction paper
   (one pastel, one bright)
scissors
glue stick
six-inch block letters for tracing the student's initials
colorful markers
pencil

Steps:
1. Trace the letters of your three initials on the pastel paper; then cut them out. Save any center pieces (from an *O*, *D*, *P*, etc.) for later use.
2. Glue just the ends of the colored strips to the bright-colored paper in a repeating pattern.
3. Weave the black strips through the colored strips one strip at a time to make a checkerboard pattern.
4. Glue down the loose ends of the black strips.
5. Apply glue to the back of the initials sheet. Glue it on top of the woven sheet (also gluing down any center pieces of letters).
6. Trim away excess ends.
7. Write or illustrate your favorite things with markers in the spaces around each initial.

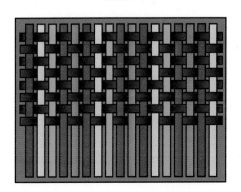

Homework Hanger

Introduce this easy arts-and-crafts project to help your students send the message that they're serious about homework! Enlarge the doorknob hanger shown to make a pattern. Then have each student trace the pattern onto a sheet of lightweight cardboard. Direct the student to cut out the hanger and write his name on the back. Collect and paint the front of each hanger with brightly colored spray paint. Allow the hangers to dry; then return them to students. Have each child use cutout shapes and glitter to decorate his hanger with a design and message to promote a quiet working area. Encourage each student to use the door-knob hanger at home to create a homework-friendly environment.

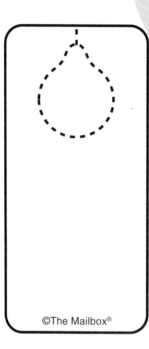

©The Mailbox®

Hobby Pizzas

Have students create their own pizzas to showcase special hobbies or interests. Instruct each student to draw and cut out a large circle from a sheet of poster board. After he decides on the type of pizza he'll make and the toppings it will include, instruct each student to boldly color in the pizza ingredients and crust using crayons. After coloring in the ingredients, the student brushes red tempera paint (sauce) over the entire pizza. The wax crayon will resist this wash. Display the completed pizzas in and around pizza boxes (donated by a local pizzeria) mounted on a bulletin board.

Patricia Green
Allen Middle School
Greensboro, NC

Clip Art

Welcome Back!

78

Dear Parent,

SCHOOL BUS

STOP

Ready or Not, Here They Come!

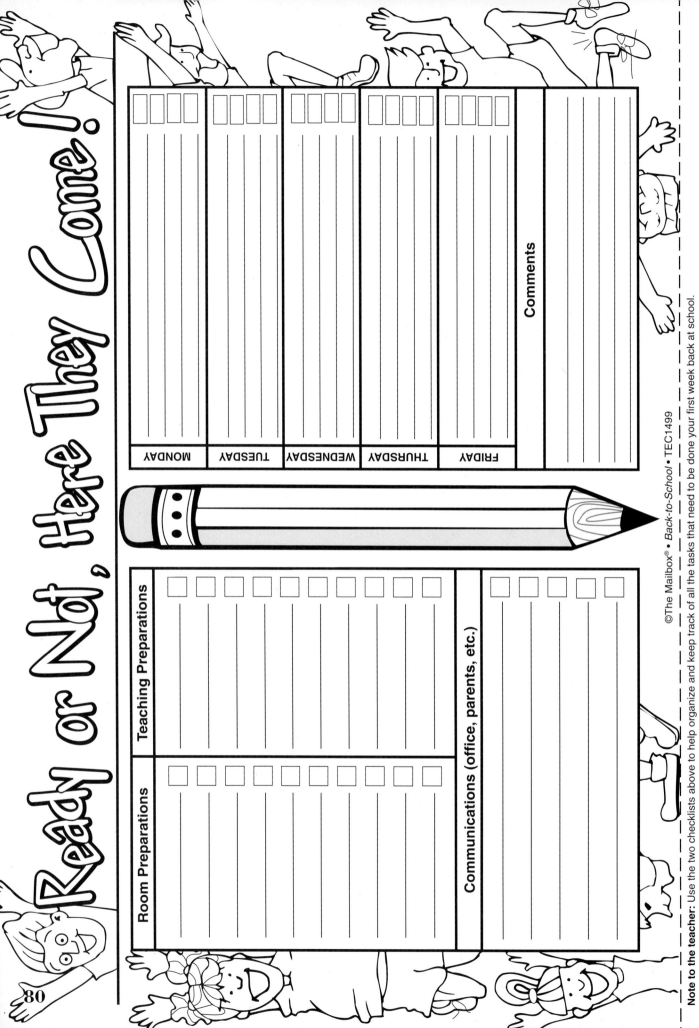

MONDAY

TUESDAY

WEDNESDAY

THURSDAY

FRIDAY

Comments

Room Preparations

Teaching Preparations

Communications (office, parents, etc.)

Note to the teacher: Use the two checklists above to help organize and keep track of all the tasks that need to be done your first week back at school.

This Week's Assignments

Name:

	Monday	Tuesday	Wednesday	Thursday	Friday
Language Arts					
Math					
Science and Health					
Social Studies					
Other					

Parent signature:

©The Mailbox® • Back-to-School • TEC1499

This Week's Assignments

Name:

	Monday	Tuesday	Wednesday	Thursday	Friday
Language Arts					
Math					
Science and Health					
Social Studies					
Other					

Parent signature:

©The Mailbox® • Back-to-School • TEC1499

Is Doing a
"Fin-tastic" Job!

Keep Up the Good Work!

Teacher: _____

Date: _____

©The Mailbox® • Back-to-School • TEC1499

Seal of Approval

Awarded to _____

for a Great Job in

_____

Teacher: _____

Date: _____

©The Mailbox® • Back-to-School • TEC1499

This certificate entitles

_____

to dive into one
homework-free evening!

Good for one subject
and assignment.

Date used: _____

©The Mailbox® • Back-to-School • TEC1499

_____

did a whale of a job on

_____!

Redeem for _____ minutes of free time.

Date used: _____

©The Mailbox® • Back-to-School • TEC1499

You're really in the swim of things!

Staple this coupon to the paper of your choice to
earn _____ points of extra credit.

Name: _____

Date used: _____

©The Mailbox® • Back-to-School • TEC1499

_____,

your work habits are "reel-y" great!

Redeem this coupon for

_____.

Date used: _____

©The Mailbox® • Back-to-School • TEC1499

Handle With Care

Dear Parent(s),

Your child's success is of the utmost importance to me as we begin the new school year. Please lend me a hand by taking a few minutes to jot down some thoughts about the following items as they relate to your child:

• special diet

• fears/insecurities

• special talents

• hobbies

• discipline strategies that have/haven't worked

• academic strengths/ weaknesses

• peer relations

• medical history/ medication(s)

• work habits

• your concerns

Note to the teacher: Distribute copies of this letter to your students on the first day of school. Ask each student to share the letter with his parents and return it to you as soon as possible.

Name(s) _____

THE GREAT BACK-TO-SCHOOL "Math-enger" Hunt

Looking for a math challenge? Work with the students in your group to find the items listed below. Write answers in the blanks provided. If you collect or make items to answer a question, store them in the envelope provided by your teacher. Work together and have fun!

1. A Scrabble game has a total of 100 letter tiles. What is the *total value* of all of the tiles?

   _____

   P₃   Z₁₀   W₄   E₁

2. Find three different grocery coupons that add up to exactly $.95.

   25¢ OFF   POPCORN   25¢ OFF

3. Find the day of the week on which each of the following holidays falls next year:

   New Year's Day _____
   Valentine's Day _____
   Fourth of July _____
   Labor Day _____
   Christmas _____

4. According to the 2000 census, what were the five most densely populated states in the United States?

   1. _____
   2. _____
   3. _____
   4. _____
   5. _____

5. Make a bar graph that shows the birthday months of all the students in your class.

6. Lines of symmetry can be drawn on four U.S. state flags. Which ones? Draw the four flags and show the line(s) of symmetry on each one.

7. What is the highest number of points scored by an individual basketball player in an NBA game? Who set the record? What team was he playing for? And when did the game take place? _____

   _____

8. List all of the factors of 2,000. (Hint: There are 20!)

   _____ _____ _____ _____
   _____ _____ _____ _____
   _____ _____ _____ _____
   _____ _____ _____ _____
   _____ _____ _____ _____

9. Scientists have identified more than 1.5 million kinds of animals, and new ones are found every year. Rank the following kinds of animals from the most found (1) to the least found (6):

   _____ birds _____ mammals _____ reptiles
   _____ fish _____ insects _____ amphibians

10. How far apart are the rails of a railroad track?

    _____

©The Mailbox® • Back-to-School • TEC1499 • Key p. 95

84 **Note to the teacher:** Have students work in groups to find the scavenger hunt items. Then have them check each other's findings.

Triple (and Quadruple) Trouble!

Mr. Jones knows he's in for a challenging year. He's just been given the names of the boys and girls who are in his upcoming class. The problem? He's discovered he will have not one, not two, but *three* sets of triplets! In addition, he'll have a set of quadruplets in his class!

Help Mr. Jones combine all of the boys' and girls' names below into a class roster. List all of the students' names in alphabetical order on the blanks provided, last names first. Check off each name as you write it. The list has been started for you.

Boys

Paul Hawkes

Austin Whitted

Thomas Brown

Josh Whitman

Timothy Brown

James Green

Bryan Billings

Scott Black

Kyle Simon

Jonathan Groth

Daniel Young

Steven Black

Mr. Jones's Class

1. *Adams, Jennifer*
2. _____
3. _____
4. _____
5. _____
6. _____
7. _____
8. _____
9. _____
10. _____
11. _____
12. _____
13. _____
14. _____
15. _____
16. _____
17. _____
18. _____
19. _____
20. _____
21. _____
22. _____
23. _____
24. _____
25. _____
26. _____

Girls

Kelsie Mitchell

Jill Green

Lisa Grove

Tiffany Brown

Melinda Briggs

Sally Black

Cassie Hartman

Amber White

√ Jennifer Adams

Stephanie Black

Becka White

Sylvia Tyson

Jessica Green

Caitlin White

Bonus Box: Alphabetize *cycle, hors d'oeuvre, gym, school, tsunami, wrangle, gnash, phrase, gist,* and *gab* by the way they are pronounced, not by their spellings. Hint: *Phrase* (frāz) is first.

Oh, Be "Cents-ible"!

How are you going to solve the problems on this page? By being "cents-ible," that's how!

Directions: Pretend that each letter of the alphabet is worth $.05 more than the letter before it: A = $.05, B = $.10, and so on until Z = $1.30. Show your work on the back of this page or another sheet of paper. Then write your answers on the lines.

1. What is the total value of your school's name? _____

2. Calculate the total value of your first, middle, and last names. _____

3. How many of your classmates have first names that are equal in value to yours?_____
   List them. _____
   _____
   _____

4. Guess which of your classmates has the most valuable first name. _____
   Why did you pick this person?_____
   _____
   Check your prediction by calculating the value of that classmate's name. Were you right?
   _____
   _____

5. Write the name of the classmate seated on your right (or left). _____
   Find the difference in the values of your first names. _____ Next, find the difference in
   your last names. _____ Then find the difference when both the first and last names are
   combined. _____ Which difference is greatest: first names only, last names only, or both
   names together? _____

6. Which school supply below do you think has the highest value? _____
   The lowest? _____ Find out by calculating the value of each item.

   a. pencil _____   e. eraser   _____
   b. crayons _____   f. bookbag   _____
   c. scissors _____   g. calculator _____
   d. glue   _____   h. sharpener _____

7. How much would your first name be worth if you multiplied the value of each of its letters by
   5? _____ By 10? _____

Bonus Box: Whose name is worth more: your teacher's or your principal's?

©The Mailbox® • *Back-to-School* • TEC1499 • written by Lori Sammartino • Key p. 95

What's My Combination?

It's time to get back in the school groove. And it's also time to learn that pesky locker combination! The combination for each locker below is made up of three numbers whose sum is 99. Choose one number from each box so that the three numbers add up to 99. Cross out each number after you use it, and write the combination on a locker. One combination has been done for you. When you're finished, you should have crossed out every number in all three boxes.

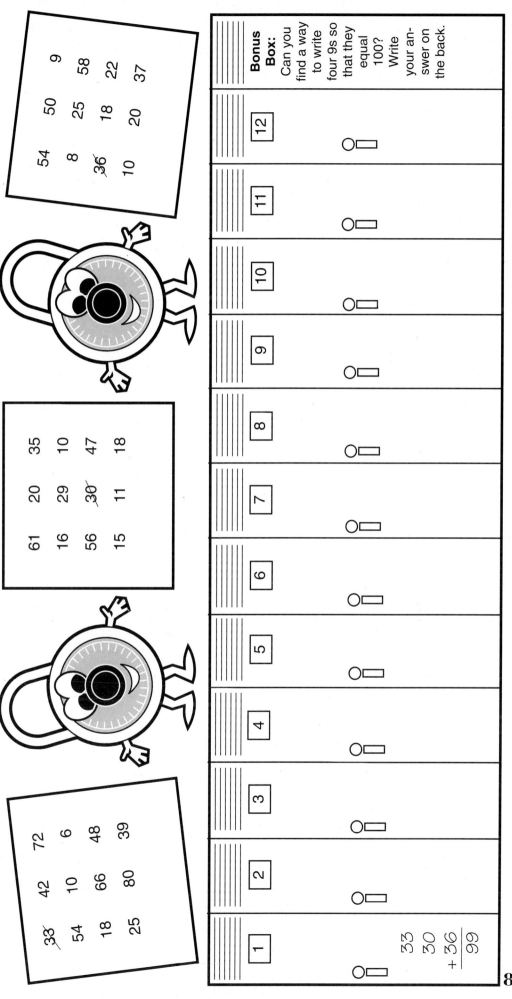

54	50	9
8	25	58
36̶	18	22
10	20	37

61	20	35
16	29	10
56	30̶	47
15	11	18

33̶	72	
42	6	
54	48	
18	66	39
25	80	

Bonus Box: Can you find a way to write four 9s so that they equal 100? Write your answer on the back.

1
  33
  30
+36
  99

2

3

4

5

6

7

8

9

10

11

12

©The Mailbox® • Back-to-School • TEC1499 • written by Ann Fisher • Key p. 95

Room Assignment Requests

The first day of school is just around the corner, and the principal still hasn't decided which teacher will be in which classroom! Use the clues and the diagram of the school below to help the principal make her decisions. Match each teacher with his or her correct room by placing a ✓ in the grid. Mark an X to show any room each teacher will not be in. Then write the room number in the blank by each teacher's name.

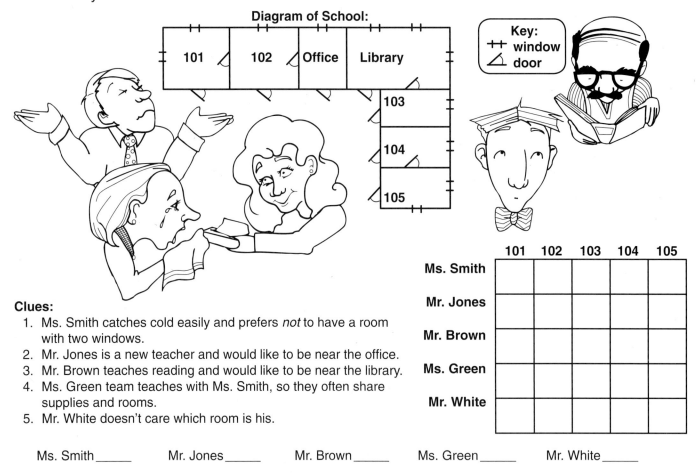

Clues:

1. Ms. Smith catches cold easily and prefers *not* to have a room with two windows.
2. Mr. Jones is a new teacher and would like to be near the office.
3. Mr. Brown teaches reading and would like to be near the library.
4. Ms. Green team teaches with Ms. Smith, so they often share supplies and rooms.
5. Mr. White doesn't care which room is his.

Ms. Smith _____   Mr. Jones _____   Mr. Brown _____   Ms. Green _____   Mr. White _____

Now that the room assignments are made, figure out which teacher will have the most and which will have the least students. Use clues to help you fill in the diagram below. Then write the teachers' names in the blanks provided.

Most Students   **Least Students**

```
 _____
|          |          |          |          |          |
```

_____   _____   _____   _____   _____

Clues:

1. Ms. Smith will have fewer students than Mr. Jones.
2. Mr. Jones will have fewer students than Mr. Brown.
3. Mr. White will have more students than Ms. Green but less than Ms. Smith.

Most Students _____   Least Students _____

Bonus Box: If Mr. Jones is Ms. Green's brother, and Mr. White is her cousin, then how are Mr. Jones and Mr. White related?

CAPTAIN CRAYON TO THE RESCUE!

Help! Someone has hidden your teacher's supplies! The start of the school year will have to be postponed unless you and Captain Crayon can crack this mystery.

Each question below contains one of the school supplies written on the crayons. Find and circle each hidden word, and color its crayon. Then write an answer on the line to show that you understand the question. Use a dictionary to find the meanings of any unfamiliar words. Let the search begin!

> **Example:** Could a bride skip gleefully down the aisle? (desk)
> **Answer:** Yes, a bride could skip gleefully if she didn't mind looking silly.

1. Would you dampen cilantro with salad dressing or motor oil?
   _____

2. Can rocks be shaped by running water as erosion occurs?
   _____

3. Can a clock erratically tick and become undependable?
   _____

4. Is it possible for a plastic ray on a toy starfish to break off?
   _____

5. Could you catch Al King trying to make a kite ascend?
   _____

6. Can a drum's tap lessen in frequency?
   _____

7. Can someone's papa steadily rise out of a chair that he has been sitting in? _____

8. Could a worksheet include a mark erroneously made by your teacher? _____

9. Should a rule resolutely remain the same for all students in a class?
   _____

10. Can music from a melodious harp energize people?
    _____

11. Can a baby play peekaboo keenly with his mommy or daddy?
    _____

12. Can a dog's rear appendage tap excitedly on the floor?
    _____

13. Would a person gape nonchalantly if he were about to step on a snake? _____

14. Would it be ethical for a taxi driver to dump a person in a chasm?
    _____

Bonus Box: Rearrange the letters from the crayon tips above to spell the name of Captain Crayon's hometown and state.

___ ___ ___ ___ ___ ___ ___ , ___ ___ ___ ___ ___ ___ ___ ___

> I love displaying your posters and pictures. I just don't like this new shade of lavender paint that was put on me over the summer!

If Walls Could Talk

It's time for school to begin, and some objects around you want to speak out before they are forgotten or taken for granted. (For example, read what the classroom wall is saying!) When you write about an object, idea, or animal as if it were human, you are using *personification.* That's easy to remember, since the root word of *personification* is *person!*

Part A

Can you figure out which classroom object is talking below? Write your answer in the blank at the end of each quote.

1. "I'm about to take a pounding. I've been pampered over the summer with cleaners and wax, but this shine won't last for long!" _____

2. "I was very quiet all summer, but I'm ready to spring into action. I have the important responsibility of letting students know when to change classes." _____

3. "Grind, grind, grind! What a workout! I'm fed 20 or 30 wooden 'sticks' each day. I chew the scraps, but I still need to be emptied quite often." _____

4. "Ouch! Although I love to have everyone admire me when the teacher is finished, it sure hurts when those staples are pushed into me!" _____

5. "I am a popular resource. I sit on a shelf in a special place so students can easily find me. I help with spelling and word meanings." _____

6. "I love to be cleaned, inside and out. I look forward to becoming a miniature 'home' for a student. I will hold her books and provide a flat surface for her to write on." _____

Part B

Now read what your sheet of paper has to say!

Hey...over here! It's me, your sheet of paper. Now I want you to practice writing dialogue. Just read and follow the directions on the right. (And one more thing: When you're finished with me, be sure to put me away in a safe place!)

1. Choose two different objects in the classroom (or outside the classroom, if you wish).

2. Pretend that the two objects are having a conversation with each other.

3. Write the conversation, including at least five lines of dialogue spoken by each object. If you want to, choose one of the samples above to begin your writing.

4. Be sure to use quotation marks and other punctuation correctly. Also, remember to begin a new paragraph each time the speaker changes.

5. As you're writing, think about what happens to each object as well as how it "feels."

Bonus Box: Choose one of the following: a kite that has lost its tail, a lone pumpkin in a pumpkin patch, or a scooter waiting for its rider. Write a brief paragraph about the item you choose, describing what it is doing, thinking, and feeling. Personify!

Back-to-School Brain Boosters

Boost your brainpower as you solve the back-to-school puzzles below.

Part A

Five friends decided to buy their school supplies as a group and then share. Each student was responsible for buying a different supply. Use the clues below to discover who bought which item. Keep track of the information given by using the chart. Put a √ in each box that is true and an X in each box that is not true.

	pencils	paper	crayons	scissors	markers
Bailey					
Biff					
Barney					
Baxter					
Bertie					

Clues:

1. Biff and Barney did not buy crayons.
2. Baxter bought scissors.
3. Bailey, Biff, and Bertie did not buy paper.
4. Bertie couldn't decide between the scented or unscented markers.

Part B

Ten students brought the same color backpacks to school. Use the clues to figure out which backpack belongs to which student. Label each backpack with the correct name.

Clues:

1. Bart's backpack is above Bob's and to the left of Beth's.
2. Bill's backpack is between Brenda's and Betty's.
3. Belinda's backpack is above Brenda's and between Bart's and Brandon's.
4. Breanna's backpack is below Beth's and they are the last ones on the right.
5. Bert's backpack is above Betty's.

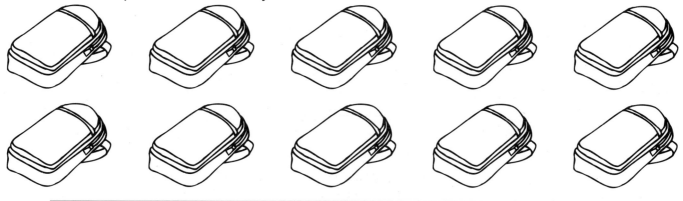

Bonus Box: Write a back-to-school logic problem like the ones above. Give it to a friend to solve.

Miss Pickwell's Puzzlers

Priscilla Pickwell takes great pride in creating puzzles to perplex students during the first days of school. See if you can solve the puzzles she's giving this year's class!

Puzzle #1

Solving this puzzle will let you in on a little secret! Start reading from one of the letters in the top row. Move to the right, left, up, or down to discover this secret. Hint: You can't move diagonally!

The secret:

I	N	B	K	S
N	G	O	O	A
R	T	S	E	R
A	O	Y	T	H
E	L	E	K	E

_____

_____

_____

_____

_____

Puzzle #2

Some schoolchildren visited the chimpanzee section at the city zoo. They gave the zookeeper this challenge: Name ten three-letter words that are chimpanzee body parts. The keeper had no problem coming up with ten words. Can you?

____ ____ ____ ____ ____

____ ____ ____ ____ ____

Puzzle #3

Use the grid on the right to rearrange the numbers in the other grid so that the same number does not appear twice in any row, column, or diagonal. If the numbers are arranged correctly, each row and column totals 100. Good luck!

0	10	30	0	40
20	20	40	20	10
40	10	30	40	0
30	0	10	30	10
40	20	0	30	20

Puzzle #4

Hidden in this puzzle is a word that completes Miss Pickwell's advice about homework. Compare each pair of numbers. Then circle the number that is greater. Write the letter above the circled number in its corresponding blank below to read the message.

	T		**B**
①	1,610	or	1,601

	W		**A**
②	27,770	or	27,707

	D		**I**
③	4,500	or	4,550

	J		**O**
④	36,005	or	36,050

	H		**J**
⑤	580,070	or	508,070

	T		**H**
⑥	882,222	or	822,882

	U		**E**
⑦	55,489	or	54,895

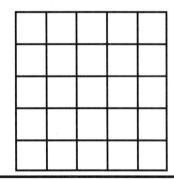

Don't Leave Home

__ __ __ __ __ __ __
2   3   6   5   4   7   1

it!

Bonus Box: When is the only time that two fours make one?

©The Mailbox® • Back-to-School • TEC1499 • Key p. 96

Back to School on Planet Zark

It's back to school for kids everywhere—even on the planet Zark! Zork (pictured below) is checking his list of supplies to make sure he has everything he needs. After all, it *is* his first day in the 8z7-894xxzth grade!

Can you decode Zork's list? Each item is written in the Zarkian alphabet, which uses the same letters that we do on Earth. The only problem is that they're in a different order! Replace each Zarkian letter with its matching Earth letter below. The code is the same for all 12 items. (Hint: The Zarkian *X* is the same as our letter *P*.)

1. XQXMA = _____

2. ATZMA = _____

3. XMUWSZ = _____

4. GQAEMA = _____

5. FQWEXQWE = _____

6. WQZWTZQBCA = _____

7. XMU = _____

8. UCBMFCCE = _____

9. MAQPMA = _____

10. WCGXQPP = _____

11. QBZQP = _____

12. HSWBSCUQAJ = _____

Code

A = ___	E = ___	J = ___	Q = ___	W = ___
B = ___	F = ___	M = ___	S = ___	X = *p*
C = ___	G = ___	P = ___	T = ___	Z = ___
H = ___			U = ___	

Bonus Box: How many words of four or more letters each can you spell using the letters in WELCOME BACK? List them on the back of this page.

Tracking Down Word Meanings

   Were these tracks made by a sleuth of bears or a gaggle of geese? Such words as *sleuth* and *gaggle* describe groups of things, particularly animals.

   Below are other words used to name animal groups. Some of the words are not used much anymore, but they do make our language more colorful and vivid.

   Write a sentence using each bold word as a group of animals. Then write a second sentence using a different meaning for the bold word.

Example: a **bale** of turtles   Joey found a *bale* of turtles near the lake.
                                    Marti fed the cows a *bale* of hay.

1. a **band** of gorillas _____

2. a **brace** of ducks _____

3. a **cast** of hawks _____

4. a **charm** of goldfinches _____

5. a **watch** of nightingales _____

6. a **gang** of elks _____

7. a **knot** of toads _____

8. a **pride** of lions _____

9. a **clutter** of cats _____

10. a **leash** of foxes _____

11. a **mob** of kangaroos _____

12. a **pack** of wolves _____

13. a **pod** of whales _____

14. a **school** of fish _____

15. a **leap** of leopards _____

Bonus Box: Make a word game with ten small index cards. On one side of a card, draw a picture of an animal group. On the opposite side of the card, illustrate a different meaning of the word. Exchange cards with a friend and try to identify the words represented by the picture clues.

        ©The Mailbox® • Back-to-School • TEC1499

Answer Keys

Page 84

1. The total value of the tiles in a Scrabble game is 187 points.
4. According to the 2000 census, the five most densely populated states are the following:
   1. New Jersey: 1,134.4 people per square mile
   2. Rhode Island: 1,003.2 people per square mile
   3. Massachusetts: 809.8 people per square mile
   4. Connecticut: 702.9 people per square mile
   5. Maryland: 541.9 people per square mile
   (Source: Bureau of the Census)
6. The state flags of Alabama and New Mexico have both vertical and horizontal lines of symmetry. Arizona's flag has a vertical line of symmetry. Colorado's flag has a horizontal line of symmetry.
7. Wilton Norman "Wilt" Chamberlain scored 100 points for the Philadelphia 76ers in a game played on March 2, 1962.
8. Factors of 2,000: 1; 2; 4; 5; 8; 10; 16; 20; 25; 40; 50; 80; 100; 125; 200; 250; 400; 500; 1,000; 2,000
9. 1: insects (about 1 million kinds)
   2: fish (about 21,000 kinds)
   3: birds (about 9,700 kinds)
   4: reptiles (about 6,500 kinds)
   5: mammals (about 4,500 kinds)
   6: amphibians (about 4,000 kinds)
10. 4 ft. 8½ in. (1.44 m)

Page 85

1. Adams, Jennifer
2. Billings, Bryan
3. Black, Sally
4. Black, Scott
5. Black, Stephanie
6. Black, Steven
7. Briggs, Melinda
8. Brown, Thomas
9. Brown, Tiffany
10. Brown, Timothy
11. Green, James
12. Green, Jessica
13. Green, Jill
14. Groth, Jonathan
15. Grove, Lisa
16. Hartman, Cassie
17. Hawkes, Paul
18. Mitchell, Kelsie
19. Simon, Kyle
20. Tyson, Sylvia
21. White, Amber
22. White, Becka
23. White, Caitlin
24. Whitman, Josh
25. Whitted, Austin
26. Young, Daniel

Bonus Box: phrase, gab, gym, gist, gnash, hors d' oeuvre, wrangle, cycle, school, tsunami

Page 86

Code for alphabet:

A	=	$.05	N	=	$.70
B	=	$.10	O	=	$.75
C	=	$.15	P	=	$.80
D	=	$.20	Q	=	$.85
E	=	$.25	R	=	$.90
F	=	$.30	S	=	$.95
G	=	$.35	T	=	$1.00
H	=	$.40	U	=	$1.05
I	=	$.45	V	=	$1.10
J	=	$.50	W	=	$1.15
K	=	$.55	X	=	$1.20
L	=	$.60	Y	=	$1.25
M	=	$.65	Z	=	$1.30

Answers for questions 1–5 and 7 will vary.
6. Predictions about which items are most and least expensive will vary.
   a. pencil: $2.95
   b. crayons: $4.75
   c. scissors: $6.05
   d. glue: $2.25
   e. eraser: $3.30
   f. bookbag: $2.65
   g. calculator: $5.30
   h. sharpener: $5.20

Page 87

Order of combinations may vary.

33 + 30 + 36 = 99	66 + 15 + 18 = 99
54 + 20 + 25 = 99	80 + 11 + 8 = 99
18 + 61 + 20 = 99	72 + 18 + 9 = 99
25 + 16 + 58 = 99	6 + 56 + 37 = 99
42 + 47 + 10 = 99	48 + 29 + 22 = 99
10 + 35 + 54 = 99	39 + 10 + 50 = 99

Bonus Box: 99% = 100

Page 88

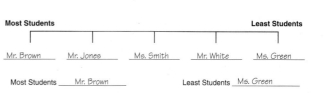

	101	102	103	104	105
Ms. Smith	✗	✗	✗	✔	✗
Mr. Jones	✗	✔	✗	✗	✗
Mr. Brown	✗	✗	✔	✗	✗
Ms. Green	✗	✗	✗	✗	✔
Mr. White	✔	✗	✗	✗	✗

Ms. Smith _104_   Mr. Jones _102_   Mr. Brown _103_   Ms. Green _105_   Mr. White _101_

Most Students ⎯ Mr. Brown ⎯ Mr. Jones ⎯ Ms. Smith ⎯ Mr. White ⎯ Ms. Green ⎯ Least Students

Most Students _Mr. Brown_   Least Students _Ms. Green_

Bonus Box: Mr. Jones and Mr. White are also cousins.

Page 89

Answers to the questions will vary.
1. pencil (…dam<u>pen cilantro</u>…)
   You would dampen cilantro with salad dressing instead of motor oil.
2. eraser (…wat<u>er as erosion</u>…)
   Running water can make parts of the earth wear away and change the shape of rocks.
3. locker (…c<u>lock erratically</u>…)
   A clock with an irregular tick is not very dependable.
4. crayon (…plastic <u>ray on</u>…)
   An "arm" of a plastic starfish might break off.
5. chalk (…cat<u>ch Al King</u>…)
   You might be able to catch Al as he's trying to make his kite fly high.
6. staples (…drum<u>'s tap lessen</u>…)
   The tapping of a drum could become less frequent if the drummer taps slower.
7. paste (…<u>pa</u>pa ste<u>adily</u>…)
   A person's papa could probably rise calmly and smoothly out of a chair.
8. marker (…<u>mark erroneously</u>…)
   A worksheet could include a mark mistakenly made by the teacher.
9. ruler (…<u>rule resolutely</u>…)
   A rule should firmly remain the same for everyone.
10. sharpener (…melodious <u>harp energize</u>…)
    It is possible for people to feel energized and renewed by listening to pretty music played on a harp.
11. book (…peeka<u>boo keenly</u>…)
    A baby is eager to play peekaboo with a parent.
12. tape (…<u>tap excitedly</u>…)
    A dog's tail could tap excitedly on the floor when his owner comes into the room.
13. pen (…ga<u>pe nonchalantly</u>…)
    A person would not stare in a carefree manner if he were about to step on a snake.
14. paper (…<u>dump a person</u>…)
    It would not be acceptable for a taxi driver to dump a person into a large crack in the earth.

Bonus Box: <u>DENVER, COLORADO</u>

Page 90

Part A

1. floor
2. school bell (or intercom system)
3. pencil sharpener
4. bulletin board
5. dictionary
6. student desk

Part B

Answers will vary.

Page 91

A.

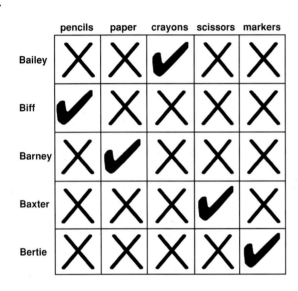

B.

   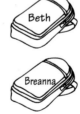

Page 92

Puzzle #1: Starting with the middle *B* in the top row is Miss Pickwell's advice: Books are the keys to learning. The arrows show the direction through the grid.

I → N	Ⓑ	K → S
N G	O → O	A
R T ← S	E ← R	
A O Y	T → H	
E ← L	E ← K ← E	

Puzzle #2: The words that the zookeeper named were *arm, ear, eye, gum, hip, jaw, leg, lip, rib,* and *toe*.

Puzzle #3:

40	10	30	0	20
30	0	20	40	10
20	40	10	30	0
10	30	0	20	40
0	20	40	10	30

Puzzle #4:

1. T
2. W
3. I
4. O
5. H
6. T
7. U

Don't leave home <u>WITHOUT</u> it!

Bonus Box: 4 ÷ 4 = 1 or ⁴⁄₄ = 1

Page 93

1. paper
2. ruler
3. pencil
4. marker
5. backpack
6. calculator
7. pen
8. notebook
9. eraser
10. compass
11. atlas
12. dictionary

Code:

A = r
B = t
C = o
E = k
F = b
G = m
H = d
J = y

M = e
P = s
Q = a
S = i
T = u
U = n
W = c
X = p
Z = l

Bonus Box: Answers will vary. Possible words include *able, amble, awoke, bake, bale, balm, beak, beam, black, blame, bleak, block, blow, bowl, cable, calm, claw, cloak, clock, comb, come, cowl, keel, lack, lake, lamb, lame, leak, lobe, lock, mace, male, meal, meek, mock, mole, wake, walk, weak, week, woke,* and *womb*.